HANDBOOK TO HIGHER CONSCIOUSNESS

Handbook

TO HIGHER CONSCIOUSNESS

KEN KEYES, JR.

LOVE LINE BOOKS

This book may be obtained through your local bookstore, or you may order it from the Ken Keyes College Bookroom, 790 Commercial Ave., Coos Bay, OR 97420 for $6.95 plus $1.50 for postage and packaging.

Fifth Edition
Twenty-fifth printing: 1988
Total printed 1972-1988: 1,000,000

Library of Congress Cataloging-in-Publication Data

Keyes, Ken.
Handbook to higher consciousness.
1. Conduct of life. I. Title.
BJ1581.2.K45 1986 158'.1 86-27785
ISBN 0-9600688-8-0 (pbk.)

LOVE LINE BOOKS
700 Commercial Avenue
Coos Bay, OR 97420

OTHER BOOKS BY KEN KEYES, JR.

HANDBOOK TO HIGHER CONSCIOUSNESS:
THE WORKBOOK

DISCOVERING THE SECRETS OF HAPPINESS:
MY INTIMATE STORY

A CONSCIOUS PERSON'S GUIDE TO RELATIONSHIPS

GATHERING POWER THROUGH INSIGHT AND LOVE
(with Penny Keyes)

HOW TO ENJOY YOUR LIFE IN SPITE OF IT ALL

YOUR LIFE IS A GIFT—So Make the Most of It!

PRESCRIPTIONS FOR HAPPINESS

YOUR HEART'S DESIRE—A Loving Relationship

TAMING YOUR MIND

THE HUNDREDTH MONKEY

PLANETHOOD
(with Benjamin B. Ferencz)

This book
is dedicated to us—
all of us five billion
human beings on earth
who, by Living Love,
can make our planet
a here and now
paradise.

CONTENTS

	Acknowledgments	ix
	Foreword	xi
1	Why This Book Was Written for Us	1
2	Secrets of Happiness	4
3	The Law of Higher Consciousness	8
4	The Twelve Pathways	12
5	Freeing Myself	19
6	Being Here Now	25
7	Interacting with Others	32
8	Discovering my Conscious-awareness	39
9	The Seven Centers of Consciousness	44
10	The Three Centers of Unhappiness	50
11	The Two Joyous Centers	61
12	The Fulfilling Centers	71
13	Five Methods for Working on Yourself	83
14	Consciousness Focusing	92
15	Techniques of Consciousness Focusing	100

16	The Instant Consciousness Doubler	110
17	Your Rational Mind	114
18	The Illusion of Self	125
19	How to Recognize Your Addictions	130
20	Living Love with Children	140
21	How to Increase Your Enjoyment of Sex	148
22	The Optimal Use of Your Biocomputer	158
23	The Programming of Happiness and Unhappiness	169
24	How to Make Your Life Work	182
25	The Purpose of Your Life	192
	APPENDIX 1 The Living Love Theory of Happiness	203
	APPENDIX 2 Summary—The Five Parts of Living Love	206
	APPENDIX 3 How to Accelerate Your Growth in the Living Love Way	209
	APPENDIX 4 Workshops for Personal Growth	212
	APPENDIX 5 Other Books by Ken	214

ACKNOWLEDGMENTS

The Living Love Way to Happiness and Higher Consciousness is a "Science of Happiness" which was formulated to contribute toward the great awakening now taking place throughout the world. As a system it is new—but many of the components that make up the Living Love Way have been tried and tested for thousands of years. This vision of the Living Love Way to happiness was made possible only by standing upon the shoulders of countless individuals who, in different places and times, have had insights into the causes of human happiness and unhappiness.

The teachings of Buddha, Patanjali, Christ, and humanistic psychology have been a constant inspiration. Others that have been most helpful are the teachings of Ram Dass, and the Buddhist teachings of Chögyam Trungpa. The teachings of Charles Berner, John Lilly, Alfred Korzybski, Krishnamurti, Pir Vilayat Kahn, and Abraham Maslow have played an important part in the author's growth. The Noble Truths of Buddha have been the fundamental inspiration for the Living Love Way to happiness.

The author is particularly appreciative of the part played in his growth by the Esalen Institute, Ed Elkin, Anatta Berner, and David and Terry Hatch (his guru-brother and guru-sister). Carolyn Terrell contributed her loving editing on the First Edition. Cas Moore did the diagram of the human biocomputer. The loving energy of Karen Zieminski and Lenore Schuh has helped in correcting typographical errors. Mark Allen, Tolly Burkan, Tony Cantea, Dorothy

Durham, Rita Gordon, Wesley Hiler, Norma Lewis, Lenore Schuh, and Allen Summers offered many valuable suggestions. Susan Stafford designed the seagull logo, and Marty Johnson did the cover drawing.

Ken Keyes, Jr.
Berkeley, California

FOREWORD

Millions of years ago when our animal ancestors had to survive in the jungle, it was necessary to have an instantly effective *fight or flight* mechanism. When a tiger was about to spring, an *automatic emotional response* was a life saver. A nervous shock was needed to squirt adrenalin into the blood so that muscles became jet powered. Emotional alarms were needed to command full attention. When a tiger was ready to jump, there was no time to admire the beautiful sunset. As a jungle survival mechanism, our animal ancestors were programmed for automatic duality—automatic feelings of otherness, threat, and paranoia. Survival required instant *domination of consciousness* to meet the perils of the jungle.

We are the pioneers in the evolution of human consciousness. It was only about 10,000 years ago that our ancestors built the first cities. As civilization grew, survival no longer depended on the instant fight or flight of the jungle. Survival and happiness now depend on tuning in to the overall situation involving ourselves, the people around us, and the total environment of the here and now. *Perceptiveness, wisdom, and oneness are now the ingredients of effective and happy living.* But our biocomputers are still programmed for jungle fight or flight—for a fast release of adrenalin into the blood stream, and for rapid heart beat—for *automatic* anger and fear. In our social interactions, our consciousness magnifies molehills and makes them into mountains—and this constant distortion destroys our energy, our insight, and our ability to love.

Thus survival in the jungle meant that we had to be programmed for instant paranoia—instant fear—instant anger—instant perception of duality. Survival in our world today means that we must have *instant perceptions of oneness—of love—of compassion with everyone and understanding of everything around us.* When we learn to cut through our paranoid jungle programming, we are on our way to higher consciousness and happiness.

Evolution is now working to remedy this primitive jungle alarm wiring in our brain that tends to hold us on lower consciousness levels. Paranoid, dualistic individuals who cannot love themselves and others tend to get heart trouble, ulcers, other psychosomatic diseases, are accident-prone, etc. Perhaps in 100,000 years, through the ruthless survival of the fittest, humans may have nervous systems that are automatically structured to produce instant insights that facilitate love and oneness. But that doesn't help you and me. We need the Living Love Way to show us how to live in higher consciousness as soon as possible—to override our jungle programming so that we can enjoy living here and now.

We have escaped from the domination of instincts (inflexible unlearned behavior) that guides animals through their daily life situations. Since the young human is not provided with a full repertoire of automatic fixed responses, we are unable to independently cope with life for a number of years after birth. This long period of plasticity and openness to learning complex life guidance patterns helps us avoid fixed preprogrammed behavior. For example, this long nurturing period lets us learn complex language systems—and our flexibility is such that we can learn to communicate in Swahili as easily as in English or any other language.

Instead of a complete pattern of animal-type instincts to provide survival responses to life situations, the young child uses ego mechanisms backed by hair-trigger emotions to develop security, sensation, and power magnification of the moment-to-moment sensory inputs. Our personal development into fulfilling, happy lives (as well as the progression of civilization beyond the dangerous power consciousness) depends on our getting free of our ego-backed, subject-object, me-them, security-sensation-power hang-ups.

It may be helpful to see this progression of consciousness in outline form as follows:

ORGANISM	METHOD OF PROTECTING AND ENHANCING THE ORGANISM
Animal	Relatively fixed life style based on instinct or unlearned preprogrammed behavior.
Lower Consciousness Human	Ego-directed, subject-object, emotion-backed security, sensation, and power consciousness (increasingly involving the rational mind) that makes us inflexibly guard and protect habitual folkways and personal patterns.
Higher Consciousness Human	The ego-driven negative emotions have been replaced by wide-ranging insight and deep intuitive understanding giving full flexibility to flow in mutually supportive and loving ways with no inflexible folkways and personal patterns.

The biocomputer with which you are equipped is the most remarkable instrument in the universe. Your only problem is to learn to use it properly. It is capable of handling two million visual inputs and one hundred thousand auditory inputs at any one time. Your biocomputer operates continually throughout all of its parts and is capable of making millions of simultaneous computations. It operates with enormous power primarily on unconscious levels—with only a tiny proportion of its activity rising to the level of consciousness. The conscious level of your biocomputer is analogous to the print-out of the man-made computers. Your journey into higher consciousness is a matter of your learning how to properly program your remarkable biocomputer. When you really learn to operate your exquisite mechanism, you will be able to fully realize your potential for a happy life.

A wonderful thing about life is that it is *naturally* good. Life is set up to work—to produce love, fulfillment, and happiness continuously. However, various situations during your first years of life conditioned you in the methods of consciousness which continually generate unhappiness in your life. *Yet every current experience can aid you in your growth toward higher consciousness if you know how to use it.*

This *Handbook* will explain how you have been creating the experiences that you have. It will show you exactly what to do to break out of the traps in your mind that are the cause of all the unhappiness that you have experienced in your life! When you apply the Methods in the *Handbook,* you will be able to turn your life around. The continuous experience of love, serenity, happiness, joy, effectiveness, perceptiveness, and wisdom that you have had only in bits and pieces can now be available to you all of the time.

You will learn how to experience the world as a friendly, loving place that has been designed to give you everything that you need. You will develop a "miraculous" quality in your life. Beautiful things will happen so continuously that you can no longer ascribe it to mere "coincidence." You will experience that you can create more love, happiness, and serenity than you need for living a thoroughly fulfilled and enjoyable life.

While this was certainly not your intention, you will become aware of how you have been turning yourself off to the energies of the world around you. Your mind has been programmed to process incoming visual, auditory, and other information in ways that continuously alienate and separate you from people. You will realize that you have been unconscious of what you have been doing to yourself. It is as though you have been born with eyes that see only with great distortion—but which give the illusion of seeing sharply and clearly. This *Handbook* will help you become aware that the only real problem in your life involves how consciously you use your mind—and it gives you clear instructions for carrying out the inner work necessary to become an energetic, perceptive, loving being.

Living Love is a positive cure for all of the suffering and unhappiness in your life and that of all humanity. The Living Love Way offers mankind one of the most powerful tools for emerging victorious in the race between higher consciousness and the suffering of atomic annihilation, ecological degradation, prejudice, and the thousand-fold ways we separate ourselves from each other.

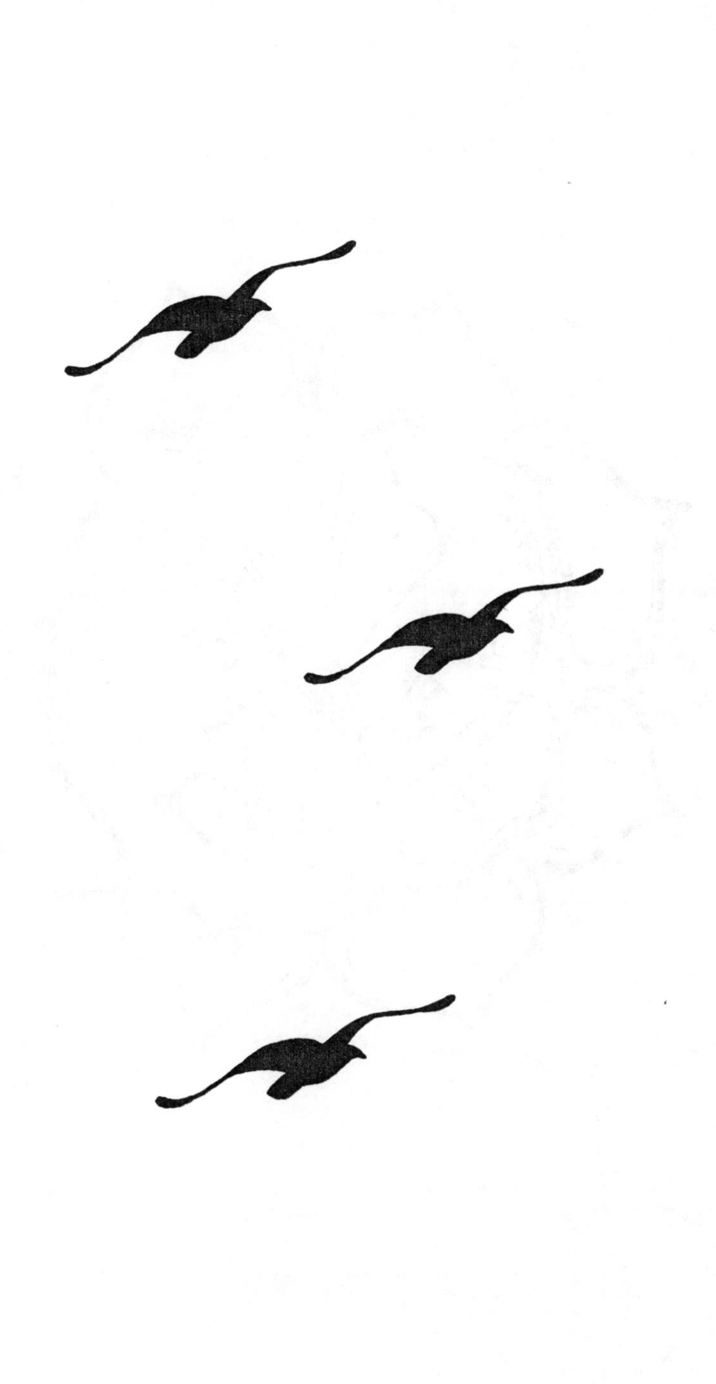

1

WHY THIS BOOK WAS WRITTEN FOR US

"Most of us," said the cosmic humorist, "go through life not knowing what we want, but feeling darned sure *this isn't it.*"

Over 99% of the people in the western world live on lower consciousness levels characterized by trying to find *enough* security, sex, pleasant sensations, ego rushes, prestige, money, power, and status. This endless struggle yields lives of constant resentment, worry, suspicion, anger, jealousy, shyness, and fear. Everything people tell themselves they must do to be happy ends up yielding more frustration than joy. The more successful a person is in making money, collecting skills and possessions, developing exciting sexual relationships, acquiring knowledge and degrees, and achieving positions of status, power, and prestige, *the less loving, peaceful, and contented he may find himself or herself.*

And yet *it is not these things in and of themselves that create an unhappy life*—it is the *internal mental addiction* or desire for them that minute-by-minute keeps one from enjoying life. Addictions (or emotion-backed demands) bring fear of non-fulfillment; jealousy that someone may steal our source of fulfillment; anger when someone thwarts us; cynicism if constantly undersupplied; paranoia if constantly threatened; boredom if we're making no progress toward satisfying our addictions; worry if we can't see a steady supply; anxiety if we're worried about being worried; and unhappiness when the outside world does not supply us with whatever it is we are addicted to. Since the nature of life is such that we win some and lose some, an addicted person has no chance of living a happy, loving, peaceful, conscious, wise, and effective life. And the addictive programming *is not necessary* to find and enjoy that which we prefer in life.

You are ready for growth into the happiness of higher consciousness when you realize the utter futility of trying to live a beautiful life by your efforts to rearrange or change the world of people and things outside of you to fit your addictions and desires. You will find you have only to rearrange your own personal, automatically programmed responses to life situations—most of which are childhood hangups.

As you work toward higher levels of consciousness, you will find that you have always had *enough* to be happy. It is the patterns in your head that make you unhappy, although you usually blame the people and conditions outside you for your unhappiness. Your journey into higher consciousness can enable you to be loving, peaceful, wise, and free of a constant barrage of unpleasant emotional feelings.

Living Love offers you four advantages in your adventure into higher consciousness:

1. *For many people* it can be one of the most powerful and rapid ways for growth into higher consciousness that has ever been available to mankind.

2. *It does not require* you to detach yourself from your present life. Living Love can be used most effectively if you stay with your present business, personal life, and other conditions until you have grown to a high enough state of consciousness to be fully perceptive of the arbitrary mores, folkways, and social roles you are guarding and living out.

3. *Once you thoroughly understand* the system, it is not essential to have a teacher for continuing your growth. Your life will be your best teacher, for you will discover that you are always putting yourself into learning situations that are ideal for your growth. The programming that you most need to change has an unerring way of putting you into life situations that can make you aware of the exact inner work you should be doing.

4. *When you use* the Living Love Way to find the love, inner peace, wisdom, and effectiveness of higher consciousness, your inner work on yourself immediately adds to your enjoyment of life. With the Living Love Way, happiness is not a distant goal—it is an ever-growing part of your here and now.

Think of the energy you now put into the up-and-down hour-by-hour coping with your feelings while you continually try to rearrange the people and situations in your life so that you can then be loving, serene, effective, and happy. And yet year by year your quest for happiness is as elusive as finding the pot of gold at the end of the rainbow. Since almost everyone around you seems to be having similar trouble in becoming a happy, loving being, you may have lowered your standards and decided that continuous happiness is probably not realistic.

The Living Love Way invites you to set the highest imaginable standards of love, serenity, peace, wisdom, effectiveness, and continuous happiness for your life. And then you are ready to begin your journey into higher consciousness.

2
SECRETS of HAPPINESS

Why do we have lives filled with turmoil, desperation, and anxiety? Why are we always pushing ourselves and others? Why do we have only small dribbles of peace, love, and happiness? Why is it that human beings are characterized by bickering and turmoil that make animals' relationships with their own species seem peaceful in comparison? The answer is so simple—but it is sometimes difficult for us to really understand because *almost every way we were taught to work toward happiness only reinforces the feelings and activities that make us unhappy.*

This is a central point that must be understood. The ways we were taught to be happy can't possibly work. Unless we see this point clearly, we cannot progress to higher consciousness. Here's why.

Most of us assume that our desires (backed up by our emotional feelings) are the true guides to doing the things that will make us happy. **But no one has yet found happiness by using emotion-backed desires as guides.** Flashes of pleasure, yes; happiness, no.

Our wants and desires are so seductive. . . . They masquerade as "needs" that must be satisfied so we can be happy at last. They lead us from one illusion of happiness to another. Some of us tell ourselves, "If I can just get to be president of this corporation, I will be happy." But have you ever seen a really happy president? His outside drama may feature beautiful yachts, Cadillacs, Playboy bunnies—but is he really happy inside? Has his ulcer gone away yet?

We constantly tell ourselves such things as, "If I could just go back to school and acquire more knowledge—perhaps get a Master's degree—then I will be happy." But are people with Master's degrees or Ph.D.'s any happier than the rest of us? It is beautiful to acquire knowledge but it is misleading to expect it to bring us peace, love, and happiness. We tell ourselves, "If I could only find the right person to love, then I would be happy." So we search for someone who our addictions tell us is the right person—and we experience some pleasurable moments. *But since we don't know how to love,* the relationship gradually deteriorates. Then we decide we didn't have the right person after all! As we grow into higher consciousness, we discover that it is more important to *be the right person* than to find the right person.

We must deeply understand why *all* of our negative emotions are misleading guides to effective action in life situations. *Our negative emotions are simply the result of an extensive pattern of scars and wounds that we have experienced.* And these emotional wounds lead us to perceive *differences* that make us uptight instead of *similarities* that enable us to understand and love. The present programming of our emotions makes us perceive other people (and the conditions of the world around us) as threats—potentially dangerous to our well-being. We then respond with adrenalin, faster heart beat, increased blood sugar, and other jungle survival responses that prepare us for fight or flight. We are trapped in our ways of perceiving the world around us.

But no one (or no situation) need be felt as an emotional threat or danger when we see things with the clearer perception of higher consciousness. Think of the most threatening situation you have felt in the last day or two. Are you about to lose your job? Is the person for whom you feel the most love paying more attention to someone else than to you? Do you have unpaid bills that you cannot take care of? Do you have a pain that could be cancer? Now, these problems either have solutions—or they don't. Either you can do something about them here and now—or you can't. If you can do something here and now about them, then do it—even if it's just a first step. It saps your energy to be worried or anxious about a problem. Do what you can do—but don't be addicted to the results or you will create more worry for yourself. If you can't do anything about a problem here and now, then why make yourself uncomfortable and drain your energy by worrying about it? *It is part of the here and nowness of your life.* That's *what is*—here and now. Worry, anxiety, or other unpleasant emotions are absolutely unnecessary—and simply lower your insight and the effectiveness of your actions.

You must absolutely convince yourself of the lack of utility of these draining emotions. You must see your unnecessary worrying as depriving you of the flowing effectiveness and joyousness that you should have in your life. As long as you think that these negative emotions have any function whatsoever, you will retard your growth into higher consciousness. If you do not hassle yourself emotionally *when the outside world does not conform with your inside programming* (your desires, expectations, demands, or models of how the world should treat you) you will have so much energy that you probably will sleep fifty per cent less. You will be joyous and loving, and really appreciate each moment of your life—no matter what's happening in the world of people and situations outside you.

Where and how did we get this emotional programming? Almost all of it was acquired in the first few years of life. For example, when we were very young, we had the experience of mother forcefully taking a perfume bottle from our tiny fingers and at the same time sending out bad vibrations based on her desire not to have her perfume bottle broken. We cried. Through being painfully pushed around, dominated, told what to do, and controlled when we were babies, we developed our emotionally intense security, sensation, and power programs. Many of our emotion-backed programs came from repeated moral directives or statements about how things "should" be. We developed a "self" consciousness with robot-like emotional responses to protect the "survival" of this separate self.

So we become emotionally programmed to feel that we must have power to control and manipulate people in order to be happy. We eventually become very finely attuned to the actions or vibrations of any person or situation that even remotely threatens our power addictions—our ability to manipulate and control people and things around us.

As we reach physical maturity and our biocomputer (or brain) is able to function more perceptively, *we have all the power we need.* But our biocomputer (backed up by the full repertory of our emotions) is still *programmed to compensate for the power deficiency* we experienced when we were infants and young children. We now need to learn to flow with the people and things around us. But our power addiction keeps us from loving people because we perceive them as objects that may threaten our power, prestige, or pecking order. If we want to love and be loved, we can't be addicted to power—or to anything else.

As conscious beings the only thing we need to find happiness in life is to perceive clearly *who we are* (we are pure consciousness and not the social roles we are acting out), and exactly what are *the real conditions,* here and now, of our lives. How basically simple is our problem! But to achieve this clear perception of ourselves and the world around us takes constant inner work. And this means developing the habit of *emotionally* accepting whatever is here and now in our lives. For only an emotionally calm biocomputer can see clearly and wisely, and come up with effective ways to interact with people and situations.

Our power addiction is only one example of the happiness-destroying programming that we put into our biocomputers when we were too young to perceive the realities of the world in which we lived. Although we now have the basic capacity for clear perception, the operating instructions we gave our biocomputer anchor us to the lower levels. And so we're unconsciously trapped.

Here and now is the reality in our lives—and it is only from the conditions of the present that our future can be generated. But our present addictions, demands, and expectations (the programming of our biocomputer) dominate our consciousness and force us to spend most of the time we are awake (and most of the time we are dreaming) in protesting and pouting about the here and now situation in our lives. This lowers our perceptiveness and keeps us from finding effective solutions to our problems. The Living Love Way to Higher Consciousness shows us how to break through this trap, to free ourselves, and to find our full potential as human beings.

3
THE LAW OF HIGHER CONSCIOUSNESS

Your growth into higher consciousness should begin by fully understanding the importance of becoming one with the Law of Higher Consciousness:

Love everyone unconditionally—
including yourself.

This law can enable you to find the hidden splendor within yourself and others. Unfortunately, we have never been taught how to love unconditionally. Almost all of our loving has been motivated by emotional desires programmed into us at an early age. Most of our love experiences have taught us we must earn or deserve love before we can have it—and that others must deserve our love. This is conditional love—it is like a barter or a business transaction. It is no wonder that our well-meaning but unskilled attempts to love usually end up in separation and alienation. We have been taught to place conditions on our love: "If you really loved me you would . . ."—and then we use one of our addictions to finish the sentence. This is an exchange—it is not unconditonal love.

What is unconditional love? It is not, "I can love you if you do what my emotional programming—my addictions—says I want you to do." It is just love. Just, "I love you because you are there. I love you because you are part of the nowness of my life. I love you because although our bodies and minds may be on different trips, on the consciousness level all of us are alike in our humanness. We are one."

Real love is simply accepting another person. Completely and unconditionally! We experience things from his or her psychic space. It is like seeing the world through his or her eyes. Whatever he or she is going through—whatever he or she is feeling—we have been there, too—at some time in our lives.

When we love, we view others as unfolding beings in their journey toward higher consciousness. We realize that no matter how intensely we strive for worldly attainments, we all seek love and oneness on the consciousness level. We are all on the journey to higher consciousness. Some of us are hearing the messages life offers us and are working *consciously* to eliminate our addictions. Others are not progressing rapidly because they do not yet know how to consciously work on themselves.

We must also learn *to love ourselves*—right here and now. We need to feel that no matter how horrible we have judged our past actions, *each day our life begins anew.* We have at all times been lovable. A child may be naughty, but he is always lovable. And so we are all children as long as we are programmed with our lower consciousness addictions. So we must accept the melodramas we get involved in as we live out our current crop of addictions. This, too, is a part of life and growth.

Every part of the system of Living Love is designed to help you learn to love everyone unconditionally—including yourself. You only need to plant the Living Love seeds in your consciousness and they will automatically sprout. Do not berate yourself because you are not enlightened by the third Tuesday of next month. The more you learn to love and accept yourself, the more you will realize that you are doing exactly what you need to do to provide yourself with experiences to grow into higher consciousness.

How can you love others if you do not love yourself? The love you have for yourself and the love you have for "another" are building blocks joining together within you to create the beautiful edifice of real love.

Learning to love unconditionally means getting free of inter-

Love
Everyone
Unconditionally
Including
Yourself

ference from our programmed addictions—those emotion-backed demanding instructions to our biocomputer. This enables us to perceive clearly what is here and now—to evaluate wisely—and to act effectively to do whatever we want to do about it. The key to this is the instant emotional acceptance of the here and now—*the emotional acceptance of the previously unacceptable.*

When our emotions are triggered, we cannot perceive clearly our actual life situation. Our biocomputer then sends a flow of information to our consciousness in which separation and alienation are emphasized. We create a horribly warped evaluation of the here and now based on our addictive programming. When this happens, we magnify differences and suppress similarities between ourselves and "others." And this destroys our ability to love unconditionally.

We all know that just having the desire to love is not enough. As far back as we can remember we have been aware of the importance of love in our lives. We know that lack of love is responsible for most of the unhappiness in the world—for difficulties in getting along with other people, for pollution, prejudice, wars, and other individual and group crimes against humanity. But what can we do about it?

The Law of Higher Consciousness suggests a practical guide for the Aquarian Age:

You add suffering to the world
just as much when you take offense
as when you give offense.

The Living Love Way to Higher Consciousness can show you step by step why you find it so difficult to love—and exactly what to do about it. The Twelve Pathways given in the following chapter tell you what you need to do to live in the Oneness Ocean of Love all of the time.

4
THE TWELVE PATHWAYS

The Twelve Pathways were formulated in 1972, and since that time they have changed the lives of countless numbers of people. The Twelve Pathways are a modern, practical condensation of thousands of years of accumulated wisdom. They give you a minute-to-minute guide for operating your consciousness while you interact with the world around you. They will enable you to live a continuously happy, conscious, loving, joyous, fulfilled life. If you've had enough of the up-and-down roller-coastering between pleasure and pain, and are really ready to enjoy and get the most out of your life all of the time, then you are ready to use and apply the Twelve Pathways to make a dramatic change in your life. In the following four chapters, we will discuss each of the Twelve Pathways in detail.

The Twelve Pathways to Higher Consciousness can show you how to accelerate your spiritual development and enable you to begin a new life of Living Love. These Pathways can show you the way to find the beauty and happiness that is hidden within you. You were erroneously taught that happiness lies in getting people and things outside of you lined up exactly to suit your desires. But our desires multiply so much faster than our capacity to satisfy them! In the Living Love System, an addiction is any desire that makes you upset or unhappy if it is not satisfied. *Life is warning you to get rid of an addiction* every time you are emotionally uncomfortable in any way.

Even if an addiction brings you pleasure, that pleasure is usually short-lived. For you will then begin to perceive *threats* to that pleasure, and you will worry about changes in your life that will deprive you of the pleasure. And you compare today's pleasure with yesterday's pleasure—and often find today's pleasure is not quite as satisfying. All of this keeps you out of the here and now. You make a giant step toward higher consciousness when you become fully aware of the price in happiness you must pay for each addiction. You can enjoy the same actions and experiences completely when you uplevel the addiction to the status of a preference.

As you become increasingly aware of how your consciousness operates, you will be able to distinguish between your biocomputer and the programming that your biocomputer uses. For example, a million-dollar IBM computer may work perfectly, but if you put garbage-type programming in it, you will get garbage-type results from this splendid machine. Computer specialists use the word "GIGO" to refer to this problem—"Garbage in - Garbage out." If you are not continuously loving everyone around you and continuously enjoying the here-and-now situations in your life, it means that your magnificent biocomputer has been operating from "garbage-type" programming. When you see yourself consciously and clearly, you realize that *you are perfect*—your only problem is to change some of the programming from which you are operating.

Your ego also plays a crucial part in the operation of your biocomputer. Based on past pleasure and pain programming, your ego selects which of the thousands of programs will be used to generate your feelings and experience of what is happening. Your ego is like a master controller that directs which emotional feelings will be triggered (joy, pleasure, anger, grief, fear, disappointment, irritation, etc.) Your ego also chooses exactly what will be projected onto the screen of your consciousness. You are aware only of what your ego permits you to be aware of. When your ego is busy reacting to the people and things around you from the lower three Centers of Consciousness, your primary awareness will be focused on what you desire and what you fear—thereby creating in

THE TWELVE

To the Higher Consciousness Planes

FREEING MYSELF

1. I am freeing myself from security, sensation, and power addictions that make me try to forcefully control situations in my life, and thus destroy my serenity and keep me from loving myself and others.

2. I am discovering how my consciousness-dominating addictions create my illusory version of the changing world of people and situations around me.

3. I welcome the opportunity (even if painful) that my minute-to-minute experience offers me to become aware of the addictions I must reprogram to be liberated from my robot-like emotional patterns.

BEING HERE NOW

4. I always remember that I have everything I need to enjoy my here and now—unless I am letting my consciousness be dominated by demands and expectations based on the dead past or the imagined future.

5. I take full responsibility here and now for everything I experience, for it is my own programming that creates my actions and also influences the reactions of people around me.

6. I accept myself completely here and now and consciously experience everything I feel, think, say, and do (including my emotion-backed addictions) as a necessary part of my growth into higher consciousness.

of Unconditional Love and Oneness

INTERACTING WITH OTHERS

7. I open myself genuinely to all people by being willing to fully communicate my deepest feelings, since hiding in any degree keeps me stuck in my illusion of separateness from other people.

8. I feel with loving compassion the problems of others without getting caught up emotionally in their predicaments that are offering them messages they need for their growth.

9. I act freely when I am tuned in, centered, and loving, but if possible I avoid acting when I am emotionally upset and depriving myself of the wisdom that flows from love and expanded consciousness.

DISCOVERING MY CONSCIOUS-AWARENESS

10. I am continually calming the restless scanning of my rational mind in order to perceive the finer energies that enable me to unitively merge with everything around me.

11. I am constantly aware of which of the Seven Centers of Consciousness I am using, and I feel my energy, perceptiveness, love and inner peace growing as I open all of the Centers of Consciousness.

12. I am perceiving everyone, including myself, as an awakening being who is here to claim his or her birthright to the higher consciousness planes of unconditional love and oneness.

you the feeling of an urgent priority. Most of these lower consciousness programs represent the urgent priorities you had at the age of two years old. Until you reprogram and change these inappropriate childhood programs, you will continually turn off the energy of the world around you that you need in order to live in a beautiful world of higher consciousness.

There are five stages in learning to use these Pathways. Each stage enables you to be progressively more aware of how these Pathways produce beautiful and sometimes "miraculous" changes in your life.

1. *In the first stage,* you are unaware of the Pathways. You are unconsciously playing out the drama of your life. You are going through your daily patterns of desiring and rejecting people and things in a mechanical and unconscious way.

2. *In the second stage,* when something happens or when someone says something that you don't like, you upset yourself even though you are aware of the Twelve Pathways. You are beginning to see how they can make your life work when you use them at the programming level where they will facilitate your interpretation of the here and now. However, you are still susceptible to your old programming which makes you automatically angry if someone criticizes you or automatically afraid if someone triggers your security addictions. The great thing about this second stage is that you are becoming aware of the lower consciousness programming that you tend to automatically run off, and you realize that there is a programming that you can use to create continuous enjoyment and happiness in your life.

3. *In the third stage* of learning to use the Pathways, you find that as soon as you are aware of any uncomfortable feelings, such as fear, anger, jealousy, grief, etc., you can pinpoint which of the Pathways you are violating. By thus engaging your rational mind and interpreting your experience by using a Pathway, you find that you progressively cut down on the period of unconsciousness in which you are a slave to your older, lower consciousness programming. In the third stage it may take several hours for you to dispel the negative emotions you are experiencing. But you now begin

to find that the amount of time that you are upset is being gradually reduced so that you experience negative emotions only for a period of minutes, or even seconds. *You can still trigger negative emotional feelings, but you are getting free from them faster and faster.*

4. *In the fourth stage,* you find that if someone does something you do not like, you may start to get angry, but at that same instant one or two Pathways flash into your consciousness. These give you an insight which does not allow the anger response to develop. You experience an increasing freedom. Your ability to love, accept, and interact flowingly with other people increases enormously.

5. *At the fifth stage,* you have eliminated all of the lower consciousness programming which triggered your negative emotional responses. You simply respond to whatever is happening here and now by using one of the Pathways (either consciously or unconsciously) in interpreting what is happening. You may be aware that you used to get angry or jealous in this type of situation, *but the feeling of anger or jealousy is no longer triggered.* You realize that you are the master of your mind, for you have determined the programming with which you want your mind to operate. This is one of the most fulfilling things that you can do.

As soon as you begin to use the Twelve Pathways in your everyday life situations, you will find that your life takes on a beautiful new dimension. Things that were previously nagging problems now become vital experiences that you confidently use in the important job of reprogramming your biocomputer. You are beginning to realize that *everything that happens to you is really perfect,* for you experience either happiness—because it fits the patterns of the programming of your biocomputer—or you experience the beginning of a negative emotion which is giving you a welcomed opportunity to work on reprogramming your biocomputer so that you will not have this problem in the future.

The Twelve Pathways are presented on the previous two pages. Memorize these Twelve Pathways in order to implant them deeply into your consciousness. Memorizing helps you use them as programming in shaping your perceptions below conscious levels.

Just reading them for intellectual understanding will not permit you to use them as dynamic tools that can make your life work. Use the Pathways in interpreting your moment-to-moment stream of consciousness. They can lead you straight into higher consciousness and enable you to find the love, happiness, wisdom, and fulfillment that is your birthright in life.

5
freeing myself

An addiction is a programming (or operating instruction to your biocomputer) that triggers uncomfortable emotional responses and excites your consciousness if the world does not fit the programmed pattern in your mind. The identifying characteristic of an addiction is that if your desire is not fulfilled, you respond emotionally in a computer-like way and automatically play out a program of anger, worry, anxiety, jealousy, fear, etc. That which you emotionally avoid is just as much an addiction as is something you desire.

FIRST PATHWAY

I am freeing myself from security, sensation, and power addictions that make me try to forcefully control situations in my life, and thus destroy my serenity and keep me from loving myself and others.

Why do addictions destroy happiness? Are there some harmless addictions? Can't I have even one addiction? Aren't there good addictions like addictions for love, knowledge, or consciousness growth?

Of course you can have one addiction—or any number you want, but for each one you pay a price in lost happiness. Since an addiction is backed up by the full rush of your emotions, each addiction from time to time puts you in a state of emotional warfare with yourself and others. They dominate your consciousness and keep you from perceiving clearly. Addictions separate you from others, for everyone is instantly valued by the degree to which you suspect threat or support. *Addictions are not needed because you can do the same things and enjoy the same life experiences on a non-addictive basis.* Through higher consciousness, you can have every beautiful experience that life offers you.

All things in the world around us are constantly changing. Our bodies and minds are constantly changing. These changes, moment by moment, month by month, year by year, affect our ability to make the flow of our life conform to the arbitrary addictive patterns that we desire and expect. So we're caught in an absolutely endless moment-to-moment struggle to make the outside world fit in with our addictions. *And it is always a futile struggle in the end.* No one that ever lived has ever had enough power, prestige, or knowledge to overcome the basic condition of all life—*you win some and you lose some.*

The operation of our lower consciousness feelings is such that even if we satisfy many addictions during a day, the one addiction that was not satisfied will prey on our consciousness and make us unhappy. There is just no way to win the battle of our addictions. There are no addictions without unhappiness, although with the higher addictions (love and consciousness growth) you experience less suffering than with the lower level addictions of security, sensations, and power.

As long as you have addictions, your exquisite biocomputer—your mind—will be dominated by the vain attempt to help you find happiness by manipulating the world around you into fitting your addictions. A mind dominated by addictions is not able to tune in to the finer vibrations of the surrounding people and things—just as a drummer who plays too loudly can keep you from hearing the violins and flutes of a symphony. To be fully here and now, you must be able to experience all of the instruments of the symphony. To live in the beauty of higher consciousness, you must be able to perceive both the grosser and the more subtle aspects of the world around you. Addictions are not evil or bad—they just cost you too much in lost perceptiveness, wisdom, effectiveness, and happiness.

Addictions always cause unhappiness sooner or later. *Preferences* never do. When an addiction is not satisfied, you are unhappy. When an addiction is satisfied, you feel momentary pleasure, relief, or indifference. When a *preference* is not satisfied, you are simply indifferent—it was only a preference after all. But when it is satisfied, it adds to the texture and beauty of your life. Your ego and rational mind do not have to guard the source of your satisfaction because you are not depending on it for happiness. *Upleveling all of your addictions to the status of preferences* (or eliminating them if they cannot add to your joy of living) is a Living Love key to being joyous and loving all the time. A practical rule of thumb for one starting on the road to higher consciousness is to grant oneself emotion-backed demands for physical necessities such as air, food if starving, or shelter if about to freeze—**and all other addictions are sickness!**

Only your emotional programming determines whether something is an addiction or a preference. You must clearly understand that when we discuss giving up an addiction, we simply mean reprogramming that part of your brain that makes you restless, churning, and unhappy if a desire is not realized. Your living patterns may or may not be changed when you uplevel your addictions to preferences. It is vital that you fully understand that the growth we are describing lies wholly in reprogramming your automatic emotional programming—it is not necessarily aimed at changing your external actions. *You can do anything you prefer as long as you are not addicted.* For when you are free of addictions, your actions will be characterized by wisdom and oneness.

Some addictions are more costly in lost happiness than others. An addiction for having money in your bank account may yield less satisfaction than an addiction for having a Ph.D. But both keep you in a constant state of threat, both dominate your consciousness, and both keep you from fully tuning in to the beautiful spectrum of the world around you. And, of course, you do not need to be addicted to money or knowledge in order to acquire them. You can prefer to have money and knowledge (or anything else) and you will then (and only then) be able to *totally* enjoy whatever money and knowledge the river of your life brings to you.

Thus it is not the *external circumstances* that constitute your addiction—it is only your *inside emotional programming* that must be changed. And the wonderful thing is that it is fully within your ability to do so—whereas up to now you have been hopelessly trying to manipulate the outside world to conform to your addictions. You will live in a peaceful world when you eliminate your addictions and then spend your time making choices on a preference basis.

SECOND PATHWAY

I am discovering how my consciousness-dominating addictions create my illusory version of the changing world of people and situations around me.

We see things not as they are—but as we are. Every addiction distorts your effective processing (on both conscious and unconscious levels) of the enormous flow of information that is continually flooding in through all of your sensory inputs. Every second your biocomputer is receiving millions of electrochemical impulses from your sight, sound, touch, taste, and olfactory receptors, and the tissues and organs within your body. For example, each hair on your body is connected by a nerve to your brain. All of your internal organs are continually sending signals to your biocomputer, most of which are fortunately handled on an unconscious level.

The reticular activating system of your biocomputer is a network that selects what goes into your consciousness. It screens the data that it sends to your cerebral center—your master analyzer. This network can close down your consciousness and put you to sleep. It can turn up your consciousness and awaken you when you are asleep. This neural structure performs the function that is often referred to as the "ego." (See Chapter 22 for a fuller discussion of neurological factors that affect your consciousness.)

You can consciously pay *full* attention to only one thing at a time although your consciousness can switch back and forth with lightning rapidity. How does your reticular activating system (or ego) select what to pass on to your consciousness? It selects the information that is to go into your consciousness by following the programming that you have been putting into it since infancy. *Thus your programmed addictions determine your experience of the world for they are the guides that your reticular activating system uses to determine which data will be suppressed and which can go into your consciousness and command full attention.* In this way, you gradually develop an illusory version of the people and things in your world because of the enormous domination of your consciousness by the things you are programmed to desire and that which you are programmed to fear.

The more you live with your distorted version of the people and things around you, the more certain you will feel that it is the only "true" picture of the world. Thus you build up a warped picture of yourself and the people and situations in your world. *For your mind is such that whatever it believes is true produces a feedback that continually reinforces and molds your perceptions.*

You should always be aware that your head creates your world. Your addiction patterns—your expectations, your desires, your attachments, your demands, your mental models—dominate your perceptions of the people and things around you. It is only when you become free of your addictive programming that you can perceive how things really interact in your world.

THIRD PATHWAY

I welcome the opportunity (even if painful) that my minute-to-minute experience offers me to become aware of the addictions I must reprogram to be liberated from my robot-like emotional patterns.

How do you spot your addictions? It's easy. You just notice the desires and expectations that you use to make yourself feel uptight in various life situations. By tuning in to your minute-to-minute stream of consciousness, you discover the addictions that make you worried, anxious, resentful, uptight, afraid, angry, bored, etc. You thus use every uncomfortable emotion as an opportunity for consciousness growth. Even though you may still be feeling emotional and uptight, you begin to get at the roots of your ups and downs—your brief bits of pleasure and your long periods of unhappiness. And you begin to feel a deep satisfaction as you become more awakened and alive!

In the past you continuously tried to find people who would minimally disturb your complex security, sensation, and power addictions. However, a person for whom you feel little attraction is probably your most helpful teacher in getting free of some of your addictions. You will grow faster if you work on your addictions by experiencing someone that you usually would have excluded from your life. When you find that you can remain centered no matter what he or she does, you will know that you have reprogrammed the addictions that created the separateness you felt. And although you have continued the relationship for your own growth, you will have offered the other person valuable experiences that he or she can use for his or her rapid growth (for example, the experience of being loved unconditionally). When you have reprogrammed the addictions that separated you in your feelings, you may have developed a love and oneness that holds you together. Or you may prefer to spend this time in another way—and it may then be more productive of growth for you to follow your preference—and be with this individual less (or not at all) in the future.

Everyone and everything around you is your teacher. If your washing machine won't work, you are being checked out on your ability to peacefully accept the unacceptable. If you are *addicted* to your appliances always working, you will suffer. If you *prefer* them to operate well, you will not compound your problem by superimposing your uncomfortable emotions on the here and now realities of repairing them.

Your moment-to-moment stream of consciousness becomes interesting and *real* when you experience everything as a step in your growth toward higher consciousness. You will soon begin to feel peaceful and loving almost all of the time. This is your consciousness telling you that you're using the Twelve Pathways more skillfully. Just keep going—you're well on your way!

6
BEING HERE NOW

One interesting aspect of the Twelve Pathways is that if you can follow any one of them completely on the deeper levels, you will be using almost all of them. They are systematically interlocking—and this makes it easier for you to implement them in action. Pathways Four through Six are particularly helpful in learning to live in the eternal now moment, although all of the Pathways reprogram you to tune in to the nowness of your life.

FOURTH PATHWAY

I always remember that I have everything I need to enjoy my here and now—unless I am letting my consciousness be dominated by demands and expectations based on the dead past or the imagined future.

If you are not enjoying every here and now moment in your life, it is because your addictions (otherwise known as desires, attachments, demands, expectations, emotional programming, models of how life should treat you) are making you dwell in the dead past or the imagined future. They are keeping you from *being here now*. All there is in your life is the *eternal now moment*—and your experience of this moment is created by the programming in your head.

Most people keep themselves on lower consciousness levels by endlessly chatting about what they did in the past or what they plan in the future. It is best not to hang out discussing the past or to let your consciousness dwell on the past, for the constant churning of your mind (and the torrent of words that issues from it) keeps you from fully experiencing the now moment in your life.

Nor will you generate the best future for yourself by being constantly preoccupied with thoughts of the future. If there is something you need to do right here now—then get busy and do it. If you've done whatever you feel you need to do at this time, then there is no need to have your consciousness filled with thoughts of the future.

The real solutions to the problems in your life will come to you when you stop hassling yourself with your addictions and become *fully tuned in* to the people and things that are around you. When your Conscious-awareness watches your own body and mind and all the people and things in the world around you from a deep, calm place inside, you will find that there intuitively wells up within you everything you need to understand. You will have insights that yield exactly what you need to do in order to flow with the river of life around you.

You can only be here now when you *instantly accept emotionally whatever happens in your life.* If you wish to change something—fine. Do it. And you can make really effective changes when your consciousness is free of emotional turmoil. You will now be more perceptive and powerful because you are able to use the full resources of your great biocomputer to flow in any direction you prefer.

For example, if a tire on your car blows out, you can get mad at the tire, angry at the people who sold it to you, resentful at the extra expenditure now necessary—or you can keep your addictions from destroying your peace and serenity. After all, the blown tire is part of the here and nowness of your life. You can only make the situation unpleasant by getting uptight. Don't be addicted to your tires not blowing—uplevel to a very natural *preference* that your tires stay inflated and serve you longer. When a tire blows, you simply accept the unacceptable. You realize that this is a here and now reality in your life. Although you have lost the tire, you do not have to lose your peace and serenity—or send out vibrations that jostle the addiction patterns of people around you and cause them tension and anxiety.

Serenity is the end—and serenity is also the means—by which you live effectively. By fully tuning in to the now moment in your life, you will discover that you always have enough to enjoy every moment of your life. The only reason you have not been happy every instant is that you have been dominating your consciousness with thoughts about something you don't have—or trying to hold on to something that you do have but which is no longer appropriate in the present flow of your life. Here and now (not pasting and futuring) is the key to the optimal interaction pattern between you and the people and things in the world around you.

The meaning of here and now is beautifully illustrated by a Zen story of a monk who was being chased by two tigers. He came to the edge of a cliff. He looked back—the tigers were almost upon him. Noticing a vine leading over the cliff, he quickly crawled over the edge and began to let himself down by the vine. Then as he checked below, he saw two tigers waiting for him at the bottom of the cliff. He looked up and observed that two mice were gnawing away at the vine. Just then, he saw a beautiful strawberry within arm's reach. He picked it and enjoyed the best tasting strawberry in his whole life!

Although only minutes from death, the monk could enjoy the here and now. Our life continually sends us "tigers"—and it continually sends us "strawberries." But do we let ourselves enjoy the strawberries? Or do we use our valuable consciousness worrying about the tigers?

Notice that the monk fully responded to the physical danger in the most intelligent way. He ran from the tigers—and he even scrambled down the cliff while hanging onto a vine. And having done this, he remained fully in the here and now to enjoy whatever life offered him. Although death was only minutes away, he did not let thoughts of the future terrify him. After doing everything he could do, he used his precious consciousness to fully enjoy every moment of his life.

There is a saying, "A coward dies a thousand deaths; a brave man only one." For all of us, death is a part of our future. But we do not have to become what the existentialists refer to as the "living dead."

We can always find things we can magnify to threaten our security, sensation, and power addictions. Or we can consciously perform whatever action is needed and then turn our attention to enjoying everything we have to enjoy. *And we always have enough to be happy if we are enjoying what we do have—and not worrying about what we don't have.*

FIFTH PATHWAY

I take full responsibility here and now for everything I experience, for it is my own programming that creates my actions and also influences the reactions of people around me.

Whenever you are unhappy, your emotions are telling you that people and things are not fulfilling the addiction patterns you have programmed into your biocomputer. But you usually do not talk to yourself in this realistic way. *Instead, you blame your unhappiness on somebody or something outside of you.* You say things like, "Mary makes me jealous," or, "Bill makes me mad." But what is really happening is that someone is doing things that do not conform with the patterns of your addictions—*and your addictions are making you unhappy.* When you take full responsibility here and now for all of your feelings and for everything that happens to you, you never again blame the people and situations in the world outside of you for any unhappy feelings that you have. You realize that it is an evasion to blame "others." You've been doing it to yourself!

You can stop being a mechanical, computer-like person who views himself as "pushed around" by the world when you realize that *only you* can "push" yourself. You begin to see the connection between your emotional programming and your suffering. You start doing something about it—which means reprogramming yourself.

Your mind creates your universe. Your expectations, demands, hopes, fears, addictions, motivations, past experience, your language system, your individual accumulation of ideas, theories, and intellectual stuff, your emotions, the structure and functioning of your nervous system and the feedback from your entire body *all interact in a complex way to produce your perceptions*—the "picture" you create from the energies you receive through your various senses from people and things around you. Your perceptions are thus a joint phenomenon of the observer and the observed.

You receive a feedback from the people and things around you that continually modifies your processing of incoming sensory data. For example, a loving person lives in a loving world. As loving individuals flow through their moment-to-moment lives, their gentle, accepting consciousness *is mirrored by the people around them*. As the Proverbs remind us, "A soft answer turneth away wrath."

Similarly, a hostile person lives in a hostile world. If you go about with rockness inside you, if you view others as competitive to you, if you have a thin surface politeness with instant anger, ridicule, and antagonism when things don't go *your* way, *you will create people around you that have exactly those characteristics*. In other words, your actions create the reactions of people around you—except when you are with people living in the Fourth (or higher) Center of Consciousness. Conscious beings remain loving and centered no matter how tense the drama around them.

The world thus tends to be your mirror. A peaceful person lives in a peaceful world. An angry person creates an angry world. A helpful person generates helpful, loving energy in others. An unfriendly person should not be surprised when he or she meets only people who sooner or later respond in an unfriendly way. A happy person finds the world filled with happy people—for even unhappy people experience temporary happiness and joy when they are with a genuinely happy and joyous person!

Sometimes people mirror you but with a reverse image. When you are addicted to one side of a polarity, you can create the opposite polarity around you. For example, if you are compulsively and addictively neat and orderly, others around you will tend to be more sloppy than usual. If, on the other hand, you are addictively sloppy, you can create neatness responses around you. The polarity of your programming may evoke an opposite ego response in the people with whom you interact.

As you grow in consciousness, you begin to realize the hundreds of ways in which you create the consciousness of everyone around you. And, of course, they reciprocally play a part in determining the contents of your moment-to-moment consciousness. This feedback of consciousness offers exquisite cosmic humor when you clearly see what is really happening. . . .

As you understand your polarities and free yourself, you begin to tune in to everyone in their deeper levels of being—where we are alike and experience oneness together. When you free yourself of your addictions, you help to free others of their addictions.

Your predictions and expectations are thus self-fulfilling. Since your consciousness creates your universe, all you have to do to change your world is to change your consciousness! It's the *only way* to live in a beautiful, joyous world. As you learn to use the Twelve Pathways to become a more loving, conscious being, you will find yourself living in an Ocean of loving, conscious beings. Without trying to change others, you will be acting in a way that is maximally effective in helping others become more loving and conscious.

SIXTH PATHWAY

I accept myself completely here and now and consciously experience everything I feel, think, say, and do (including my emotion-backed addictions) as a necessary part of my growth into higher consciousness.

The Living Love Way to Higher Consciousness is based on the *instant emotional acceptance* here and now of that which you previously regarded as unacceptable in your life. Acceptance simply means that you won't cause yourself emotional conflict because of your current perceptions. Emotional acceptance doesn't mean that you have to continue living the rest of your life with any particular person or situation. You are free to do anything you prefer to do—but don't be addicted to the results of your actions. If someone does something that "hurts your ego," you will grow fastest *if you consciously regard him or her as your teacher* who is enabling you to discover which addictions you will have to reprogram.

You really savor living when you consciously experience everything that you feel and do as taking place in the theater that we call our world. You see yourself and others as actors in the daily drama of life. But the real *you* is not your body or mind. You're not the actor. *The real you is your Conscious-awareness.* And your Conscious-awareness is just digging the whole show from the audience. Shakespeare wrote,

All the world's a stage,
And all the men and women, merely players;
They have their exits and their entrances,
And one man in his time plays many parts.

When you watch the entire drama of your life and that of other people from the safe vantage point of the audience, you begin to provide a distance that enables you to see your addictions more clearly. You will find it easier to completely accept the addictive dramas that you have to play out on the stage of your life. You will find a turned-on joy in consciously experiencing everything as a necessary part of your growth into higher consciousness.

To grow in the Living Love Way, you do not have to drill yourself and criticize yourself with military precision. Just experience everything in an accepting, relaxed, and *conscious* way—and realize that every one of your experiences is perfect for your here and now growth into higher consciousness. Your addictions will gradually fade away when you use the Living Love Pathways to *consciously* interpret your moment-to-moment stream of consciousness. *Don't push the river—just experience the river consciously* from the vantage point of the Twelve Pathways.

7

INTERACTING WITH OTHERS

Flowing—not manipulation—is the way of higher consciousness. Flowing means moving with the forces around us—being in tune with the vibrations of the people and things in our environment. Flowing enables us to find the love, beauty, and peace that we are missing in our lives. But flowing is impossible based on the models of how to be happy that we learned in our childhood, for we cannot flow or harmonize when we are the slaves of our addictions. Our addictions force us to manipulate ourselves—and others. As adults whose minds and bodies have completed their structural growth, we have the potential of flowing in the river of our lives in a beautiful, loving way.

SEVENTH PATHWAY

I open myself genuinely to all people by being willing to fully communicate my deepest feelings, since hiding in any degree keeps me stuck in my illusion of separateness from other people.

As you begin to uplevel all of your addictions to the status of preferences (or eliminate them entirely), you will discover that you no longer have anything to hide from other people. It then feels good to be able to communicate with each person exactly what you are experiencing. As you grow into higher consciousness through eliminating your addictions, you will be able to drop all deceptive, subject-object manipulation in the games you have been playing —the money game, the security game, the male-female game, the prestige game, the power game, the knowledge game, the expert game, etc. These can be beautiful games to play when you play them consciously and lovingly, but they generate suffering and unhappiness when you play them addictively.

When you are not completely open and truthful to all people—when you are trying to hide a part of your inner feelings—you continue the illusion of separateness from others. Hasn't everyone been caught up in the addictions for security, sensation, and power? Are you under the illusion that you have desires and feelings that are so horrible that others will be shocked? Or are we really all one? Deep inside, all of us have experienced this self-imposed suffering and isolation that keeps us from being peaceful and loving—even though we may not have perceived it as self-imposed. We have all been in similar predicaments at one time or another in our lives.

One of the ways out of this wall of isolation is to communicate, "Well, here I am. This is what my addictions are making me feel here and now. I accept myself (including my addictions) as being on an unfolding journey toward a peaceful, loving state of higher consciousness."

When you're around someone who is experiencing fairly continuous states of higher consciousness, you can be sure that he or she will unconditionally accept you exactly where you are now—for he or she has travelled over the same road and prefers to help you. You can grow fastest and enjoy the trip most (even though your remaining addictions make it a bit rocky sometimes) if you can relax and just communicate fully.

It feels so good to be able to just open up and let people see all of you. You'll be amazed at how quickly they can then cut through their drama and accept you without the phony masks and roles with which you previously identified. You have every right to feel exactly as you feel. If "others" are bothered, that's their problem. You're their teacher giving them experiences they need to reprogram their addictions—just as they are your teacher enabling you to find your addictions.

When you consistently use the Pathways, you do not have to scream, viciously attack, or otherwise unduly threaten another person in order to communicate your deepest feelings. You don't need to lay judgments on people or prove them wrong. You just talk about your own consciousness. Instead of, "You are horrible and I don't want to ever see you again," you can say, "You've put me in touch with one of my addictions, and right now I feel so angry at you I don't want to be with you." When you just talk about your own consciousness, you give both yourself and the other person a better chance to work through the addictive programming that produces the illusion of separateness.

The Ninth Pathway suggests that you give yourself a short period of time to work through the emotion caused by your addiction. But if you are at the beginning of your consciousness growth, you may find it more important to communicate quickly so that your relationships are always "up front." Remember, *hiding separates; openness unites.*

As you grow into higher consciousness, you will become aware of the many ways in which you have been involved in complex role playing, with hidden "shoulds" and "shouldn'ts" that create complicated patterns of demanding and expectation. You can work effectively toward the "us" space when you genuinely and openly communicate your feelings and reveal the security, sensation, and power dance that you have been doing. You will find that you can usually cut through these ensnaring dramas by expressing your preferences clearly to yourself and others. You will realize that open communication of your innermost feelings helps your ego (and the egos of other people) to get free of addictive programming which in the long run only produces unhappiness and alienation.

EIGHTH PATHWAY

I feel with loving compassion the problems of others without getting caught up emotionally in their predicaments that are offering them messages they need for their growth.

All your emotional problems are created by your addictions. Your growth into higher consciousness consists of becoming free of these traps. When you interact with people who are still involved in this automatic computer-like emotional programming, it is important that you learn to feel their problems with loving compassion, but without getting caught up emotionally in their predicaments. Compassionate understanding—yes; pity and commiseration—no.

Compassion means that when you empathize with the predicaments of other people, you silently send out the vibration, "Yes, I know. I've been there too. It's OK to feel the way you do—however, try to see that it's all drama. Life always has its 'tigers'—and we do what we can about them. But above all, let's be sure to continuously enjoy the 'strawberries.' There are always enough strawberries to enjoy our here and now *if we don't put all of our attention on the tigers!"*

Compassion means that you understand the duality and separation they are creating in themselves by rejecting what is here and now in their lives—but you do not get caught up in their poignant drama. Compassion means that you realize that you can do the most for other people when you stay centered and high and loving whenever you are around them for they are playing out their addictions, suffering because of them, and hopefully picking up the messages life is offering them. Compassion means that you love and serve them from a clear love space, and not from a compulsiveness or guilt motivated by your remaining security, sensation, or power addictions.

You learn not to give gifts that you cannot emotionally afford to give. When you resent helping someone, this creates obligations, duality, and separation. You cannot psychologically afford to give such help, and the recipient cannot afford to receive it. The price in personal distance and separation is too high if you give to avoid a feeling of "guilt" or from a "should" or "ought" motivation.

When you help someone because of a feeling of obligation or duty rather than free-flowing love, you may find yourself resenting the person for needing your help. These negative feelings can prevent you from being sensitive to his or her real here-and-now needs, and doing or saying what would really be helpful. Very often just being in a loving space with a person as you listen to him or her is more helpful than any advice you could give.

When you can "help" someone with a feeling of love and oneness—*you just do it because it feels good to you.* When you feel oneness with another, *there is no giver or receiver—there's just us here.* It's like one hand washing another. You are just letting energy flow through you.

When you are with someone who is trapped in the suffering caused by addictions, you use this as an opportunity to work on your consciousness. The greatest thing you can do for "others" is to remain happy and loving when you are with them. You do not get caught up as a supporting actor no matter how tragic the role they are playing in the drama of their life. It's their thing to play this role. They probably chose this role (either consciously or unconsciously) and are clinging to it. The best way to give them a chance to free themselves from their addictive trap is for you to avoid getting caught up emotionally in the "stuff" that they are taking so seriously. They are not that "stuff" with which they are identifying. Behind all that, *here we are.*

As the Law of Higher Consciousness suggests, the game is to "Love Everyone Unconditionally—Including Yourself." As you begin to increase the number of people for whom you feel unconditional love, you will be aware of the many security, sensation, and power dramas that each of them is busily playing out. You realize that you cannot, in practice, have enough time and energy to love everyone you meet if you have a "bleeding heart" response to the heap of problems people are creating in their lives.

Your life works best when you love, serve, and flow your loving energy—not from a lower consciousness motivation of "I am helping you," or "I will save you," but simply from the awareness that "the universe gave this energy to me and it feels good to pass it along." As you become more conscious, your energy will increase. And also, as you become more conscious, less of it will be drained by your own security, sensation, and power addictions. You will then liberate a continuous stream of energy which will flow into loving and serving people around you.

NINTH PATHWAY

I act freely when I am tuned in, centered, and loving, but if possible I avoid acting when I am emotionally upset and depriving myself of the wisdom that flows from love and expanded consciousness.

When you are emotionally upset, you energize the addictive patterns of other people who are also caught in the lower levels of consciousness. They will mirror your uptightness, and will not be tuned in, perceptive, and able to fully understand what you are trying to tell them. They will reflect your inner conflicts, for you will trigger their addictions—and this will interfere with effective communication. The things you do or say when you have stirred up your emotions and the emotions of other people will be handled in a way that is destructive of peace, love, and oneness. You may be able to pull a power trip to make something happen—but it will not feel right to all concerned. And the future consequences of your actions will cause greater future conflicts.

Bad vibrations, like the measles, are contagious. Every time you interact with anger, resentment, or fear, you add a little reinforcement to the addictions from which we wish to be liberated. You know the story of the man who bawled out his friend, and the friend went home and fought with his wife, who spanked her child, who then kicked the cat.

Now let's turn it around—for good vibrations are also catching. Let's be the man who complimented his friend, and the friend went home and kissed his wife, who was so extra loving to her child that he gave the cat some milk without even being asked!

To avoid adding to the total sum of the bad vibrations in the world, unless you are in physical danger, wait until you are tuned in, centered, and loving before you act. Then your perception and wisdom may lead you to choose a more effective course of action. But even if you do the same thing that you originally intended to do, it now has a better chance of success because *the consciousness level of everyone concerned is elevated.* Instead of acting out a drama of addictions, you are, here and now, communicating as a tuned-in human being telling what you feel and what you prefer.

The Seventh Pathway and the Ninth Pathway put you in an interesting predicament. The Seventh Pathway tells you to communicate your deepest feelings, and the Ninth Pathway says for you to withhold your communication, if possible, until you are perceptive, centered, and loving. What this means is that you are always ready to be completely open and to communicate with people, but if you are caught in the grip of a disturbing emotion, you give yourself a little time to work on your addiction—rather than acting out the fight-or-flight feeling you have triggered.

A part of your growth into higher consciousness will be associated with how perceptively you handle these two Pathways. You can use the Ninth Pathway to hide—or you can use it to delay your responses to people long enough to give the other Pathways an opportunity to rescue you from the negative emotions you have triggered. Always remember that you cannot put off for long your making an up-front communication of your deepest feelings if you wish to be conscious, perceptive, and loving. Unexpressed feelings act like a cancer in your brain that malignantly spreads—warping your perceptions and bringing you alienation and suffering. You thus learn to use the Seventh and Ninth Pathways to create more and more aliveness and beauty in all of your relationships with other people.*

* *Prescriptions for Happiness* by Ken Keyes, Jr. gives three simple techniques to bring more insight and love with other people: Ask for what you want—but don't demand it; accept whatever happens—for now; and turn up your love—even if you don't get what you want. For more information, see Appendix 5.

8
discovering my conscious-awareness

The Twelve Pathways give you a complete solution to every emotional problem in your life. Whenever you experience uncomfortable emotional waves, you will find that the Pathways are always ready to steer you around the rocks into the peaceful waters.

TENTH PATHWAY

I am continually calming the restless scanning of my rational mind in order to perceive the finer energies that enable me to unitively merge with everything around me.

When our wonderful biocomputers are dominated by our addictions, our consciousness is scattered and harried. Our consciousness is then like a television set that drifts from the channel, that turns off when we want to use it, that sometimes won't stay turned off when we wish to sleep, that is subject to fading, and that will tune in only the lower channels. We would not tolerate this type of performance from a television set, but unfortunately most of us are so accustomed to the poor performance of our minds that we often accept such inefficiency as "normal."

What is meant when the Tenth Pathway tells you to calm the restless scanning of your rational mind? As you grow in awareness, you will begin to realize that the activity of your rational mind is generally sparked by your security, sensation, and power motivations. You are trying to hold onto something you do have, get something you don't have, or avoid something you don't want. You discover how your rational mind has become a pawn commanded by your ego to "rationalize" your security, sensation, and power demands and expectations. You begin to see that many of the "clever" things your rational mind devises to say to other people just turn out to be separating and alienating responses that keep you out of the "us" space.

As you lessen the heavy load of addictions you have been carrying, your rational mind becomes quieter and quieter, and you begin to increase your insight and perceptiveness. You begin to have a choice that was not available before regarding the things that you say and do. You begin to tune in to the finer energies around you when the precious space on the screen of your consciousness is not occupied by the emergency alarms triggered by your addictive security, sensation, and power models of how the world should be.

The Living Love Way enables you to live in this powerful realm of higher consciousness by setting you free from your addictions, goals, and expectations that you have *unknowingly programmed as essential to your happiness*. For the structure and function of your biocomputer are such that this addictive programming triggers your thoughts, ideas, and words in a persistent and dominating way.

The cultivation of preferences (in place of addictions) does not keep your rational mind churning and scanning—for preferences are not sought after goals that keep you restless. With preferences, you simply flow along in the nowness of your daily life. Whenever the here and now offers you a choice, you pick the one that most fits in with your preferences. But either way—everything feels all right. Your rational mind is not excited into restless, striving activity. Preferences let you stay in touch with the here and now in your life. They enable your mind to become calmer and calmer—until it functions as a powerful, quiet, one-pointed, peaceful, effective servant to your consciousness.

Thus the Living Love System enables you to transcend tensions, anxiety, and conflict into a flowing acceptance of all of life. Your escape from lower consciousness levels helps to free you from the restless scanning of your rational mind so that you are constantly in touch with that deep, calm place inside of you from which you peacefully, lovingly, and blissfully watch the drama of your life.

ELEVENTH PATHWAY

I am constantly aware of which of the Seven Centers of Consciousness I am using, and I feel my energy, perceptiveness, love, and inner peace growing as I open all of the Centers of Consciousness.

The Seven Centers of Consciousness (explained later in this book) consist of a seven-step scale that can tell you each moment of your life exactly where you are in your journey toward higher consciousness. By using the seven-step consciousness scale, you clarify your minute-to-minute drama and add realism and depth to your life. You discover that your energy, love, insight, and inner peace will fluctuate up and down when your consciousness is involved in the lower three Centers. As you learn to uplevel your consciousness, you unlock enormous energy. You enjoy being able to unconditionally love and accept everyone. By letting yourself grow toward the higher Centers of Consciousness, you find the beautiful inner peace that you have always sought in your life.

In Living Love we work to integrate all of the Centers. *Everything in your life has aspects on all of the Centers.* You begin your growth toward higher consciousness when you first escape from being preoccupied with the lower three Centers of Security, Sensation, and Power—and uplevel your consciousness to include the unconditional Love Center and Cornucopia Center. Then you begin to watch your drama from the Conscious-awareness Center. By seeing your drama from this meta-center you impartially witness all your thoughts and actions on the five lower Centers. In the next phase of consciousness growth, one goes behind this Conscious-awareness Center into the Seventh Center—Cosmic Consciousness—that peaceful place where one has eliminated personal boundaries and has unitively merged with the surrounding world.

TWELFTH PATHWAY

I am perceiving everyone, including myself, as an awakening being who is here to claim his or her birthright to the higher consciousness planes of unconditional love and oneness.

Everyone you meet, including yourself, has the capacity for clear perception, wisdom, effectiveness, peace, and love. *We are equal beings*. But unless one has consciously worked toward higher consciousness, this hidden splendor within may be smothered by the addictive games that keep one separated and isolated. It will help us in our journey to higher consciousness (as well as being most helpful to others) if we regard everyone, including ourselves, as fellow travellers on the road to awakening.

We begin to realize that everything we do is *either a skillful or unskillful attempt to find love and oneness.* Even if someone yells at you or hits you, he is trying to manipulate you so that you can fit the pattern of his addictions—and thus permit him to love you in his conditional way. When your ego permits you to see the here-and-now actions of people with perspective, you realize that there is practically nothing that anyone can do that you have not either done or wanted to do at some time in your life. *We're just not that different from each other.* Our egos and our rational minds keep us continually judging other people so as to put them in the wrong and thus give us a supposed advantage. A conscious being simply sees, with a compassion that is born of insight and perspective, that everyone is on the road to awakening. We learn to love others by accepting and loving ourselves—and *vice versa.*

You realize that in place of the judgmental terms (such as good and bad) that we use to separate ourselves in our consciousness from each other, the simplest and most helpful ethical standard is to see things as degrees of separateness and oneness. You view *the thoughts and actions that separate you* on the lower part of the ethical scale. *The thoughts and actions which unite you* are on the upper part of the scale. Instead of labeling things "good" or "bad," you simply use your insight to determine to what extent your thoughts or actions separate or unite you *in your feelings toward others.* That which makes you feel separate tends to keep your life from working effectively, and that which enables YOU to experience love and unity permits you to harmonize your energy with the energies of the world around you. Whenever you are in doubt about whether to do something or not, just ask yourself *whether it makes you feel more separate from people or more loving toward people.*

When you see how it all is—when you see everything that happens in your life as a moment-to-moment acting out of the great drama of your addictions—you will realize how you constantly smother the potential that you have within you. Higher consciousness means that you experience a flowing harmony with all of the interacting people and things in the world around you. This permits you to emotionally accept whatever is here and now in your life. Higher consciousness is not a mystical, metaphysical, far-out state. It is a practical, beautiful state of mind which is your birthright as a human being.*

*** *How to Enjoy Your Life in Spite of It All* by Ken Keyes, Jr. allocates an entire chapter for each Pathway. It shows you how to apply them in everyday life situations to increase love and happiness. For more information, see Appendix 5.**

9
THE SEVEN CENTERS of CONSCIOUSNESS

In the Living Love System, we use a seven-step scale that will enable you to measure your pattern of growth toward higher consciousness. This scale consists of three lower Centers of Consciousness—Security, Sensation, and Power—and four higher Centers of Consciousness—Love, Cornucopia, Conscious-awareness, and Cosmic Consciousness.

These Centers act as filters that generate *your particular private experience* of the here and now in your life. Information coming into your biocomputer—from your eyes, ears, and other sensory receptors, plus the memory banks of the brain and the thoughts generated by the rational mind—are processed through these programmings. *These programmings determine your own unique experience of the here and now.* The emotional areas of the brain trigger various feelings as called for by your addictive programming. This in turn feeds back and intensifies your particular flow of energy and thought patterns.

The lower three Centers of Consciousness were developed for survival in the jungle phase of the evolution of our species. In general, the automated priority of awareness in an animal is to first check incoming information for its security aspects, then its sensation (food or sex) possibilities, then its threats to the power boundaries with which the animal identifies. For example, a cat may be operating on the sensation level enjoying a meal when an unexpected noise may instantly activate a security consciousness that prepares the animal for fight or flight. All this is done on an *automated basis without conscious thought.*

In spite of the fact that the potential for higher consciousness is available to us as we leave childhood, we often remain trapped in these automated responses of security, sensation, and power consciousness. For example, when we use our security programming, we *automatically* trigger the experience of fear. If we don't get the sensations we desire, we *automatically* trigger a frustrating disappointed feeling. And if our power, pride, or prestige boundaries are violated—like automatons—we instantly trigger the experience of anger, hostility, irritation, hate, etc. We often combine two or more of these filters simultaneously to create our individual picture of the now moment.

One of the benefits of the seven-step consciousness scale is to enable you to see your drama from a perspective so that you can choose the filters you wish to use in generating your experience. This conscious choice of programs is not available to a young child or an animal. Young children and animals are trapped in their automatic programming. To see your drama clearly is to be liberated from it, so that you do not have to compulsively act out the subject-object scripts of your jungle ancestors.

A beautiful aspect of the consciousness scale is that each time you go up a step in the scale, your life gives you:

1. **More energy.**
2. **More contact with people.**
3. **More enjoyment.**

An important characteristic of the three lower Centers is that you can never get enough to enjoy your life continuously when you are using the security, sensation, and power filters to interpret the here and now in your life. You can use these filters to make limited improvements in your life. But out of the billions of people who have lived on earth, no one has experienced *enough* security, *enough* delightful sensations, and enough power to be continuously happy and fulfilled. The experience of *enoughness* only starts as you begin to generate your consciousness more and more from the Fourth Center—the Love Center.

The reason why the lower Centers cannot bring you *enough* is that they cause constant distortions in perceiving people and life situations. These Centers keep you from loving unconditionally and make you relate to people as objects instead of as beings just like you. They make you waste energy compulsively running toward or away from situations. These lower Centers subject you to simultaneous, multiple addictions that conflict with each other and require the biocomputer to do something about the heavy emotional overload. When overloaded with conflicting addictive demands that are not being satisfied, the experience of the here and now is grayed over with repression, anxiety, depression, and dullness. These emotions are used by your biocomputer to slow you down and keep you from tearing yourself apart with conflicting demands, desires, and expectations generated by your security, sensation, and power consciousness.

It should be remembered that life in a jungle frequently poses the threat of instant death to its animal inhabitants. We have a beautiful white cat that purrs and is most loving to the people in our house. When this cat goes out into the yard, however, it will crouch down, stalk, and kill birds if it can. The automated response patterns of any nearby birds must be able to handle the life or death aggressiveness of the cat when it plays out its jungle programming.

We have nervous systems that were evolved over millions of years to cope with this immediate threat to life. It has probably been quite a long time since you or I were actually threatened with immediate death. But these mechanisms of fight or flight that were so protective in the jungle are still operating in our biocomputers. They may be helpful if you were in a boat that overturned and you had to swim one mile to a nearby island. This threat to your life, when processed by your lower three Centers of Consciousness, would bring about autonomic nervous system responses that would enable you to swim in a way that you've never been able to swim before. But in over 99% of your normal daily interactions with people and life situations around you, these fear, disappointment, and anger emotions are not helpful in enabling you to get the most enjoyment and effectiveness from your life. For example if someone criticizes you, your angry response will tend to bring you additional criticism—"stuff" you might avoid if you could just consciously hear the criticism and perhaps ignore it, if inappropriate, or use it if it fits.

The Seven Centers of Consciousness should be used as growth tools—and not as another way to criticize yourself or to generate an experience of inadequacy or inferiority. You do not need to fiercely attack yourself because you caught yourself on level three when you decided to spend the day on level four. No part of the Living Love System should be used addictively to create expectations that make you drive yourself, berate yourself, complain about yourself—or anyone else.

The Living Love Way works best if you simply stay with it and notice in a quiet, accepting, meditative way where you are from moment to moment. And remember, where you are is perfect for your consciousness growth—you shouldn't be anywhere else—here and now. You simply notice what is happening in your moment-to-moment stream of consciousness as seen from the vantage point of the Living Love Way. And each time you use one of the Living Love Methods, you will find that you are becoming more peaceful and loving in a situation that previously would have resulted in your emotionally thrashing around and upsetting yourself and others.

On the next page you will find a summary of the Seven Centers of Consciousness. It will help you if you will learn the seven-point scale so thoroughly that you will feel (without necessarily analyzing it) which Center of Consciousness your biocomputer is operating on at each moment.

In the next three chapters you will find detailed descriptions of each Center of Consciousness.

THE SEVEN CENTERS

1. THE SECURITY CENTER.

This Center makes you preoccupied with food, shelter, or whatever you equate with your personal security. This programming forces your consciousness to be dominated by your continuous battle to get "enough" from the world in order to feel secure.

2. THE SENSATION CENTER.

This Center is concerned with finding happiness in life by providing yourself with more and better pleasurable sensations and activities. For many people, sex is the most appealing of all sensations. Other addictive sensations may include the sound of music, the taste of food, etc.

3. THE POWER CENTER.

When your consciousness is focused on this Center, you are concerned with dominating people and situations and increasing your prestige, wealth, and pride—in addition to thousands of more subtle forms of hierarchy, manipulation, and control.

4. THE LOVE CENTER.

At this Center you are transcending subject-object relationships and are learning to see the world with the feelings and harmonies of flowing acceptance. You see yourself in everyone—and everyone in yourself. You feel compassion for the suffering of those caught in the dramas of security, sensation, and power. You are beginning to love and accept everyone unconditionally—even yourself.

# of consciousness

5. THE CORNUCOPIA CENTER.
When your consciousness is illuminated by this Center, you experience the friendliness of the world you are creating. You begin to realize that you've always lived in a perfect world. To the degree that you still have addictions, the perfection lies in giving you the experience you need to get free of your emotion-backed demands. As you reprogram your addictions, the perfection will be experienced as a continuous enjoyment of the here and now in your life. As you become more loving and accepting, the world becomes a "horn of plenty" that gives you more than you need to be happy.

6. THE CONSCIOUS-AWARENESS CENTER.
It is liberating to have a Center from which your Conscious-awareness watches your body and mind perform on the lower five centers. This is a meta-center from which you non-judgmentally witness the drama of your body and mind. From this Center of Centers, you learn to impartially observe your social roles and life games from a place that is free from fear and vulnerability.

7. THE COSMIC CONSCIOUSNESS CENTER.
When you live fully in the Sixth Center of Consciousness, you are ready to transcend self-awareness and become pure awareness. At this ultimate level, you are one with everything—you are love, peace, energy, beauty, wisdom, clarity, effectiveness, and oneness.

10
THE THREE CENTERS of UNHAPPINESS

There is nothing about any level of consciousness that is right or wrong, good or bad, pure or evil. You should feel free to let your consciousness touch on any of the seven levels. You are where you are—here and now. Your growth in Living Love will depend on completely accepting yourself and others—right here now—and not in some future time when you have conquered your addictions.

Just accept where you are now by realizing that you are experiencing addictions that give you the feelings you need for your next step in growth. By joyously using your here and now as a stepping stone, your growth will be happening in the fastest possible way.

Here is the Living Love scale you can use to develop a moment-by-moment feeling of where you are in your great adventure into higher consciousness:

THE FIRST CENTER OF CONSCIOUSNESS—THE SECURITY CENTER

What is it that makes you feel secure? What is it that makes you feel insecure? Your answer to these questions is probably misleading to you, for your feelings of security are created by your emotional programming—what you are telling yourself inside. The outside conditions of your life do not make you feel either secure or insecure. *They only trigger your inside programming.* One person may feel secure with practically no money at all. Another may feel insecure with a million dollars in the bank.

The Security Center automatically triggers feelings of fear and anxiety when the outside world does not conform to your security programming. Observe how much of your time is involved in an unpleasant striving to achieve the conditions that you tell yourself you must have to feel secure. The Security Center of Consciousness is very demanding and strongly pulls your consciousness away from the higher Centers.

You will escape being trapped in this first level of consciousness when you begin to understand that your feelings of security or insecurity are due to your emotional programming which you picked up from addicted people before you were mentally and physically mature. You will also notice the impossibility of getting *enough* of whatever it is that you equate with security. You may be like the rat who is running as fast as he can in a revolving cartwheel cage. *There is no way to get there by running faster—or by achieving more efficiently.*

Paradoxically, you would probably be safer if you never again experienced fear in your life—unless you were actually trapped in a jungle situation faced with the need for immediate fight or flight on a physical level. You will be far safer when *consciousness replaces the emotional response of fear.* For example, if you wish to cross a busy street, you increase the probability of being hurt if you are afraid of being hit by speeding automobiles. You will be safest if you are simply conscious of the automobiles running back and forth and calmly wait on the curb until there is a break in the traffic. When you perceive this break, without the slightest experience of fear, paranoia, or danger, you calmly and peacefully walk across the street. If you were totally unconscious of what happens when an automobile hits you (as a small child is), fear would be helpful to make you more aware of the overall situation. But once you are old enough to be conscious of the various factors involved in a life situation, a fear response makes you more jumpy and less perceptive, it uses up your energy by making you tense, and it keeps you from enjoying your here and now.

A loving person lives
in
a loving world
A hostile person lives
in
a hostile world

Everyone you meet
is your mirror

It is interesting to note that most of the time in your present adult life, the experiences of insecurity and fear are usually associated with the "futuring" of your rational mind. You will be apprehensive and worried about what may happen next. You tend to forget that in all of the situations that you went through last year, you were, in the here and now, able to handle them in one way or another. If you look back over all of the "threats" of the past year, you may be able to develop the understanding that you did not need fear or feelings of insecurity to produce the optimal response to each situation in the here and now of your life. In fact, all of the fear and worrying that you did simply wasted your energy and potential for happiness. Some of us manage to kill almost all of our enjoyment of the present by worrying about the future. If there is something you need to do to make you more secure in the future, then you get busy and do it. That's here-and-now action. But if there is nothing you can do, the game is to let it go from the screen of your consciousness. Tell yourself that if the problem comes up as a here-and-now reality, you will have the energy, perceptiveness, and loving help that you need to respond to it optimally. If you work on reprogramming your security addictions by using the Living Love Methods, you may be able to become sufficiently conscious so that you will never again experience fear in your life. This is the beginning of "freedom."

The Security Center is such a lonely level of consciousness! When your consciousness is preoccupied with striving toward what you feel to be your "security needs," you are more isolated from people than on any other level. And your energy will be at its lowest. When you are preoccupied with security, you trap yourself in subject-object relationships with others. You create "others" as objects to help you become more secure—or as objects to fight because they threaten your security. On the security level you cannot love "others" since this level creates great distances between you and other people. If your consciousness is imprisoned on the security level, you may sleep from nine to twelve hours a day and still complain of being tired. When you are no longer hung up on the Security Center of Consciousness, you may sleep less than six hours a day and feel energetic and refreshed.

You transcend the security level by developing a deeper and deeper understanding of how your hunger for "security" is all a matter of your emotional programming. It is a trip that you are doing on your own head. Your feelings of insecurity are not a necessary consequence of people, things, and circumstances around you. You will begin to realize that your life right now *is what it is*. And if you eliminate your addictive models of how things should be, you always have enough to feel good right here and right now.

If you prefer to make changes in your life, you can make them far more effectively when you transcend the addictive programming that makes you feel insecure. When your consciousness begins to operate more and more in the Love Center and Cornucopia Center, your higher consciousness will enable you to flow into situations that offer you far more real security than your lower-consciousness struggle for "security" will ever provide. For real security lies only in the love and flowing that you will discover through higher consciousness. It can never be found in manipulating the world of people and things around you.

THE SECOND CENTER OF CONSCIOUSNESS—THE SENSATION CENTER

A person who is hung up on the Security Center of Consciousness tells himself, "I can be happy if I can just feel secure." However, once he begins to feel more secure, he finds that this is not quite true. He then feels that if he can arrange the people and things in his life to provide a constantly varied pattern of beautiful sensations, he will be happy.

If you are like many people, sex may be your most sought-after sensation. Your life style may be designed to provide you with sexual sensations. The people you choose to be with, the clothes you buy, the home you live in, and the style of speech, thinking, and action that you have developed will tend to be determined by whatever you calculate will make you appeal to the sexual partners you most desire. This is known as subject-object sex in which you are the subject and treat "others" in your life as sexual objects.

There is nothing wrong with doing this except that you are operating on a level of consciousness that cannot provide happiness. For sex is never enough. You are tuning in to only a small part of yourself—and even a smaller part of others. They are not responding to you as a whole person and you are not responding to them as a whole person. Behind the exquisite sexual dance, both of you really feel the shallowness of the subject-object relationship. You know something is wrong, even though you don't know exactly what it is. Because no matter how many terrific sexual orgasms you may have, they are never enough. Even if you could reach sexual climaxes a dozen times a day, *life would still seem hollow.* For this second level of consciousness can only produce flashes of pleasure and long periods of indifference and boredom.

Sensations, however pleasant, can never make you happy if you are depending on them for happiness. You become driven, thwarted, sometimes satiated, and not tuned in to the flow of the here and now when you are chasing sensation after sensation. *But the same sensations can be totally enjoyed when your consciousness is no longer stuck on the second level.* When your consciousness is primarily tuned to the Love Center or the Cornucopia Center, sensations can add to your happiness as a part of the here-and-now flow of your life.

Although sex is the sensation that many people are most heavily addicted to, it is by no means our only addiction on the Second Level. We tell ourselves that we can find happiness through the taste of food, the sounds of music, the experience of a special environment that we regard as our impressive home, the sensations of movies and plays, etc. The search for happiness through sensations keeps us ingeniously busy—but nothing is ever enough—until **you are enough.** When you are enough through higher consciousness, everything can be enjoyed as part of the great drama of your life. Until then, nothing ever quite does it for you, and the enjoyment you seek will tend to elude you as long as you addictively demand it. When you uplevel addictions into preferences, you enjoy it all.

When your consciousness is primarily directed toward providing you with the sensation patterns to which you are addicted, you will have more energy than when it was hung up on the Security Center of Consciousness. You will usually be with more people and you will need to sleep less. An individual who is hunting for sex is definitely generating more energy than a person who is worried about his security. In fact, one who is heavily addicted to the security level will probably have dropped off to sleep during the early part of the evening. Thus the search for happiness through sensations is definitely an improvement over the search for happiness on the Security Center of Consciousness. But wisdom, peace, and serenity are not yet in sight.

THE THIRD CENTER OF CONSCIOUSNESS—THE POWER CENTER

The last of the lower Centers of Consciousness (that can never provide you with "enough") is the Power Center. Most of the people in the world are addicted to these three lower Centers—the Security Center, the Sensation Center, and the Power Center. The attempt to find happiness through the Power Center is definitely a forward step in growth toward higher consciousness. When you are operating from the Power Center, you will have more energy and you will interact with more people. But these will still be subject-object interactions in which people either cooperate with your power games or threaten them. In this Center, life is a series of competitive moves and countermoves.

What do you strive for on the Third Level of Consciousness? Is it money as a method of wielding power rather than money as a form of security? Is it prestige—because the more prestige you have, the more you can manipulate people? Do your power addictions keep you preoccupied with external symbols such as a mod car, an attractive home, fashionable clothes, etc? Or have you upleveled the game to internal status symbols—such as knowledge and lots of hobbies so that others perceive you as an interesting, achieving person? Or perhaps sex has now become a power game whereby you enjoy sex not only for the sensations but also as a challenge to your Power Center. Do you seek the sexual partner who is hardest to attract because of the ego challenge?

Have you ever noticed that the people who are the most successful in the power game are simply living a hollow life with external evidences of worldly success—but without really winning inside in terms of peace, serenity, and oneness with others? It often happens that the more successful a person becomes on the outside, the less successful he is on the inside. Anxiety, ulcers, and heart disease tend to increase with external "success."

To the degree that your moment-to-moment consciousness is biased by security, sensations, and power, you are trapped in the lower consciousness folkways of our culture—and you are not finding enough in life to be happy. You are ready for your next step toward higher consciousness when you deeply realize the *utter futility* of trying to make it in life using these lower consciousness levels. This does not necessarily mean that you must drastically change *your external activities.* For what you renounce is your addictive demands and not necessarily the things you are doing. For example, it is not money or sex that causes unhappiness—it is your addictive demands for money or sex. It is the clanging of the emotion-backed circuits in your biocomputer that keeps you disappointed, frustrated, and suffering if the happenings outside you do not exactly correspond to your inside programs. Thus you do not renounce your worldly activities—for it's all here for you to enjoy. You renounce your emotion-backed demands which keep you from enjoying the bountiful life that has always been available around you.

It is easy to see the more obvious power games involving money, political power, status symbols, people bossing each other around, etc. But it is helpful to be aware of the more subtle power games we play. For instance, it is clear that someone talking in a loud voice may be trying to control people, but a power game may also be present when someone talks in an unusually soft voice that makes people be quiet and listen hard if they are to hear. Someone who is constantly ordering people around and who forcefully insists that people accept his or her opinion can be coming from the Power Center. However, someone who is always quiet can be subtly manipulating by his or her "sweet acceptance" and "you-always-know-best" attitude. This type of subtle manipulation makes one put energy into extracting what someone else really wants. This game creates a subject-object type of separateness. We might ask ourselves, "What do I do to get what I want?" "What masks do I wear?" "What part in the drama do I play?"

You have hundreds of things in your head that you are now protecting as a part of your personal boundaries and social position. You will grow in happiness as you gradually realize that all of this stuff is not who you really are. It's just ego-backed programming that you picked up on your way to where you are now. Your energy will enormously increase and your sleep needs decrease as you give up guarding the various manifestations of your security, sensation, and power addictions.

One of the bonuses of higher consciousness is that when you give it all up, you get it all back. What you give up are your inner addictive demands—what you get back is more of everything than you need in order to be happy. As you grow into the Fourth Center of Consciousness, you will find that you have all the power you need in your life—in fact you will have more than you need. For your unconditional acceptance of everyone around you will open doors that you could never have opened when you operated from the Third Center of Consciousness.

When you approach life with power addictions, you will be instantly resisted by the power addictions of other people. Instead of opening themselves to help you get what you want, they close themselves and are automatically antagonistic to your power thrusts which threaten them. As you grow into the higher Centers of Consciousness, you will begin to experience an effectiveness that you could never attain when you were shoving from the Third Center, trying to bulldoze life into giving you what you thought you needed for happiness.

Some of the most dramatic performances of your ego and your

The Three Lower Centers Produce Unhappiness in Life

CENTERS	ASSOCIATED EMOTIONS	WHY THE THREE LOWER CENTERS OFFER A YO-YO TYPE OF ENJOYMENT OF LIFE
1 - SECURITY	Fear, worry, anxiety, etc.	1. Constant driving compulsiveness. 2. Constant fear of loss. 3. The rational mind can always trigger an unlimited chain of future possibilities to worry about.
2 - SENSATION	Disappointment, frustration, boredom, etc.	1. Constant driving compulsiveness. 2. Constant fear of loss. 3. When we repetitively experience an enjoyable sensation, we become satiated and bore ourselves.
3 - POWER	Anger, resentment, irritation, hostility, hate, etc.	1. Constant driving compulsiveness. 2. Constant fear of loss. 3. Our power threat stimulates a counter-attack from others and we are continually caught up in defending and trying to control.

rational mind will be triggered at the Power Center of Consciousness. Some methods of consciousness growth treat the ego and rational mind as enemies to be destroyed. In the Living Love Way, we regard the ego and the rational mind as friends that are really there to help us—but they can be like ignorant friends who hurt us as often as they help us. Helpfulness requires both skill and understanding. Our egos and rational minds are often like the well-meaning neighbor who sees his friend lying in the street with a broken spine after being hit by a car. When he picks him up to take him to the hospital, the broken spine crushes the spinal nerves so that his friend will never walk again. In trying to help, the neighbor ignorantly damages his friend. Similarly, when our egos and rational minds use lower consciousness programming, they continually keep our lives from working in ways that produce optimal enjoyment.

The Living Love Way does not try to kill your ego or your rational mind. Since they are our friends that would like to help us, *we engage them to help us root out our addictions and uplevel them to preferences.* We realize that our egos trigger a feeling of uneasiness when the outside world does not fit our addictive models of how it all should be. They also give us a flush of pleasure when the outside world does fit our addictions. In either case, we need our egos to give us the emotional experiences that enable us to become aware of our addictive demands—and to understand the heavy price that we pay for all of them sooner or later if they are not reprogrammed into preferences.

The goal is not to kill your ego—*but to retire it due to lack of work.* If you killed your ego, you might retreat into a schizoid-type shell that would keep you from enjoying the beautiful things life offers you. Your ego has a vital part to play in revealing to you the addictions you have yet to work on. When you reprogram your addictions, your ego will automatically stop triggering negative emotions that interfere with your happiness. So welcome your ego, *watch its operation,* and use it as a necessary part of you that will give you the experiences you need in order to grow into higher consciousness.

11
THE TWO JOYOUS CENTERS

In the previous chapter, we saw that the Security, Sensation, and Power Centers of Consciousness cannot be depended upon to continuously enable you to feel that you are getting "enough" to be happy in life. One problem with the Security Center is that, with a little imagination, you can always find one more loophole in your security setup that must be plugged. And there is no end. . . . The Sensation Center of Consciousness cannot work to produce happiness for you either, because you will very likely become bored with anything that you do repetitively. You seek to solve the boredom trap by finding more and more variety, but this in its turn just brings another set of problems into your life. The Power Center of Consciousness will not work to produce happiness for you because your pushing, dominating, and manipulating will stimulate similar actions from other people. Their defensive and offensive tactics then require you to be more dominating and forceful, but this only works for a short while until the people outside of you respond with even more force. What you expected to be a simple solution to a situation actually sets up the next round of problems in your life. When you see the unconscious dance in which you have been ensnarling yourself, you begin to realize that a higher Center of Consciousness is required to enable you to enjoy your life.

In the last chapter we learned that when our consciousness operates on the lower three Centers of Security, Sensation, and Power, we can achieve great external success—but be a failure inside in terms of happiness. We are beginning to get somewhere in our journey toward awakening when our consciousness deals more and more with the drama of our lives from the point of view of the two joyous Centers—the Love Center and the Cornucopia Center.

THE FOURTH CENTER OF CONSCIOUSNESS—THE LOVE CENTER

The Fourth Center of Consciousness in the Living Love Way is called the Love Center. *Love comes with the unconditional acceptance of everyone and everything around us.* And how do we do this? When your consciousness lives in the Love Center, you instantly accept anything that anyone does or anything that happens—but the acceptance is only on an emotional basis. You're still entitled to your preferences. A mother will love her child even though he upsets the quart of milk and it smashes on the kitchen floor. She prefers that the quart remain intact. But if it spills, that's here and now. Why get emotionally upset and bother herself and the baby too?

How do you love everyone unconditionally so that you do not upset yourself—no matter what he does or says? You can do this only by transcending your security, sensation, and power addictions—for it is only your emotional programming that disturbs you when the events outside do not conform with the programming that you have conditioned inside of you. As your addictions begin to melt away, you begin to experience everything and everyone around you in a different way. You view them not in terms of how they meet your addictive needs—for you are losing those "needs"—you just view them in terms of, "Well, that's what is—here and now." You realize that each individual has the need to be doing exactly what he or she is doing—here and now. You realize that everyone (including yourself) is creating a world in which one's addictions are lived out. When you consciously notice the hollowness and suffering that these addictions cause, you achieve insights that help you get free from them.

You are in the Love Center when you accept everything people do as part of their journeys toward awakening. You know that if they are consciously on the path, they will similarly accept your moment-to-moment "stuff"—for this is what helps them grow, too. And if they are not consciously on the path and become angry, that's their problem. As your addictions become upleveled to preferences, you begin to find that you can instantly accept what was previously unacceptable emotionally. After all, you really have no choice. Whatever is—IS!!! That's where it's at—right here and now. You might be able to change the situation one second, one minute, one hour, or one day from now. And by not getting irritated, you will be more effective in realizing your preferences.

As you learn to live more and more in the Love Center of Consciousness, you will begin to find that you are creating a new world in which your consciousness resides. People and conditions are no longer a threat to you—for no one can threaten your preferences. "Others" can only threaten your addictions. And you're losing them fast. Soon your mind will create no "others."

As your addictions are reprogrammed, you will find that your "ego" has less and less to do, and your ego will activate the egos of other people less and less. Thus people begin to experience you as becoming purer as you give your ego less to do. This helps them become purer. Even though they may still be stuck in the lower three Centers, they find that they seldom get in touch with tense feelings when they are with you. They can begin to get a taste of what it is like to live in the more joyous Centers of Consciousness. They may come down when they are not with you, but you will have planted a seed of awakening.

When you live more and more in the Love Center of Consciousness, you will find that your blood circulation will improve—and your hands and feet may be warmer. Your blood vessels will no longer be tight and restricted so that you feel cold excessively and deeply. Your face and the back of your neck and head will stay especially warm and glowing. Your skin will experience cold but you will not feel cold inside. This is one of the beautiful physiological things that happens as you grow into higher consciousness. This greater openness of your circulatory system also affects your brain and other organs to make them function more effectively. Colds and illness become rare.

As you spend more and more time in the Fourth Center of Consciousness, you will find that you enjoy touching people more and more. Now that you are seldom paranoid you can enjoy the beautiful feelings of warmth and oneness that you can experience when you make contact not only through words, sight, and sound, but also through your touch receptors. As you break through the illusion of duality and separation, you begin to realize that it was *only your head* that previously kept you from loving people unconditionally. It was *not their actions* as you had been conditioned to believe.

You begin to see with insight the worldly dramas of addictions that people are still playing out on the first three levels of consciousness, and you feel compassion toward those who still are involved in the illusion of separateness. You know that the best way to help them is to work on yourself so that they can perceive (perhaps for the first time in their lives) the experience of unconditional love. They begin to say to themselves, "Wow, here is someone who accepts me all the time—no matter what I do or say." Love doesn't require you to get involved in their "stuff," as they struggle through life seeking security, sensations, and power. You just accept them because they are there—because they have a right to be there—and because where they are is perfect for their growth—and also yours.

Every experience you have of other people either leaves you peaceful and loving or it makes you aware of the remaining addictions to be reprogrammed. When someone does things that you previously found unacceptable but which you can now emotionally accept, you can say to yourself, "Great! I'm getting on with it. Joe just checked me out and I passed the test of being free of that addiction." There is nothing wrong with letting your ego give you a little pat on the back because you are living more and more in the Love Center. You use your ego to constantly raise your Center of

Consciousness. If Joe does something and you make yourself feel a bit uptight and alienated from him you can say to yourself, "Joe is my teacher, because he is showing me an addiction that I should get rid of."

In the Fourth Center of Consciousness, you experience "work" as an expression of love and caring. "Work" is no longer performed unconsciously or mechanically with the feeling that one can fully enjoy life again when the job is done. You will increase your growth into higher consciousness by learning to flow energy into meeting the needs of "others" as though they were your own needs. To paraphrase an ancient saying, "When I don't know who I am, I SERVE everyone around me; when I do know who I am, I AM ONE with everyone around me."

Selfless service is a beautiful way to get free of the three lower Centers of Consciousness. An ego grasping for security, sensation, and power will always trade or barter energy for something that will best enhance its mirage-like lower consciousness situation. *When you do only those tasks that are pleasant, unavoidable, or that enhance your security, sensation, and power trip, you let your ego keep you trapped.* Selfless service without thought of reward is a characteristic of the Fourth Center of Consciousness.

You are beginning to experience that living in a world of love is always *enough.* You know that your feelings of isolation, separation, and paranoia are always artificially created by your emotional programming. You realize that although our bodies and minds are different, in the realm of Conscious-awareness all of us are the same.

And just as a mother loves her infant no matter what he does, you realize that as you grow into higher consciousness you can love everyone around you—regardless of what he or she says or does. Even if someone attacks you fiercely through words or even hits you, he is simply playing out his addictions. He is trying to get you to act differently so that his addictions will not trouble him when he interacts with you.

So no matter what happens, you experience *everything* as

love. You finally arrive at the place where nothing that happens in the world around you knocks you out of the Love Center of Consciousness. You can emotionally accept everything. You can always return love no matter what a person does or says. And by doing this, you will be doing the most you can to help others transcend their addictions. If you remain loving even when they try to hurt you, they may begin to find that love place in themselves which they so want to experience—but which they don't yet know how to find. Everything is either an effective or ineffective way of creating love, peace, and oneness.

No matter how horrendous your acts may be, you always want to be understood and loved. So does everyone else. So just remember how we are trapped by our addictions. And then you will understand. And then you can unconditionally love everyone as an unfolding being.

Relationships that are held together by "shoulds" or "shouldn'ts" lose their spontaneous here-and-now vividness. Love cannot be a programmed addiction held together by fear or pressure. Real love blossoms and remains where there is no addiction—but instead a vibrant, totally here-and-now involvement. And the optimal future is always generated from the free-flowing, non-expectant present moment.

If you have current obligations, you acknowledge these and follow through with them. For when you begin your journey to higher consciousness, you start from where you are right now. When you ignore or avoid your obligations, you create a "me-them" attitude. This does not create a space for the harmonizing of energies into an "us" consciousness. And as you consciously relate to your obligations, you *work them out by working on yourself.* In the future you make only those obligations which you can flowingly fulfill within an "us" space.

When you live in the Love Center of Consciousness and are relatively free of addictions, you will find that you can love everyone unconditionally. **For it is your involvement that is conditional—not your love.** You have only twenty-four hours in a day, and your time will usually be spent with people who have similar preferences and with whom you enjoy doing things. When the deep-

HAPPINESS
happens
when your
consciousness is
not dominated
by addictions
and demands—
and you
experience
life—
as a
PARADE
OF PREFERENCES

est harmonizing of energies takes place between people, they enjoy just being together. It is not necessary to continually keep up a heavy drama of activities—you can just silently be with each other and totally enjoy being in each other's space. You may do many things together—but the doing is never compulsive or contrived. You are able to experience a deep inner peace by simply being in each other's presence. And you are able to love everyone around you, but you do not necessarily become involved in the dramas of everyone.

When two people love from the Fourth Center of Consciousness, they do not experience the love they have for other people as detracting or threatening the love they share. They are not held together by a jealous, romantic model of love that constitutes an addiction that makes them vulnerable to suffering. They keep their consciousness in a state where they are totally involved—and yet totally non-addicted. They give each other total freedom and unconditional acceptance. They love and serve each other in a relatively egoless way. Equally for both of them, loving and serving yields the maximum of all the beautiful things that life can offer.

As you experience the peace, harmony, and love that you are creating in your life, you begin to realize that all of the problems in the world will solve themselves when we four billion people on earth live in ways characterized by love and service. You know that every feeling that you have, and every thought and communication you make, can add to the world total of loving energy that can in chain-fashion propagate itself forever.

THE FIFTH CENTER OF CONSCIOUSNESS—THE CORNUCOPIA CENTER

As you live more and more in the Love Center of Consciousness, you will open yourself to more people and life situations. Instead of shying away from people and situations as you have done in the past, you now realize you have nothing to be afraid of. You will begin to find friendships that you could never have found before. You will discover yourself exploring areas of life that you would never have experienced previously because of your security, sensation, and power addictions. You now experience them in an open, relaxed way—rather than in a preconceived, judgmental way. You will be *1000% more open* to various experiences that are available to you than when you were making choices based on the lower three Centers of Consciousness.

This openness is beginning to let you flow and experience life in an almost miraculous way. Since you are open, most life situations which were a problem to you now find beautiful solutions. Events are seen in terms of results and happenings instead of people's supposed attitudes toward you. People who have things to teach you (but from whom you closed yourself off) can now come into your life. Since your ego has less and less work to do as the slave of your addictions, you are beginning to experience the whole spectrum of your here and now. Your perception has increased enormously. You now have higher predictability in your thinking. Because you have created a beautiful, peaceful world in which you now live, you are helping everyone around you find the beautiful, peaceful place inside. And you can accept help without feeling that an obligation is created.

You will begin to experience your life as one "miraculous" happening after another. But this transformation could have happened at any time in your life—because you have created it simply by your constantly increasing *openness* to people and things around you. You begin to see that the miracle was always there, but it took place in its own court—because you were too busy hassling yourself with your addictions and trying to manipulate people and things around you. Life is now offering you a Cornucopia or a "Horn of Plenty."

And the "miracle" of Cornucopia consciousness occurs because of three powerful factors that *automatically aid you when you substantially reduce the number of addictions you are guarding:*

1. *Since addictions waste your energy,* you will now have *a huge supply of energy* to use as you prefer.

2. *Since addictions blind you,* you will now have *clear insight* into what you should do or not do in various life situations.

3. *Since addictions separate you from others,* you will now live in a *loving energy field* in which people love you and help you.

As you gain insight into the Cornucopia Center of Consciousness, you will begin to feel that you live in a *friendly world* that will always give you "enough" when you live in the higher Centers of Consciousness. You will also begin to deeply feel that you live in a *perfect world.* You will not feel it as perfect from the limited point of view of your instant happiness when you have addictive programming. But your world is perfect from the point of view of continually providing you with precisely the life experiences that you need for your overall development as a conscious being.

A paranoid person feels that everybody is trying to keep him from getting what he needs to be happy. The world is a giant conspiracy to hurt him. The Fifth Center of Consciousness represents the opposite of paranoia. In this Center you experience people and situations around you as part of a generous world that constantly offers you everything you need to be happy.

You will begin to live more and more in the Cornucopia Center when you experience deeper and deeper aspects of your world as a *friendly,* nurturing place. You feel at home everywhere.

Who could ask for more? And yet there is more as you grow toward the last two Centers of Consciousness.*

*** *Discovering the Secrets of Happiness: My Intimate Story* by Ken Keyes, Jr. shares his process of consciousness growth in going beyond the Security, Sensation, and Power Centers into the Love Center. See Appendix 5 for more information.**

12
THE FULFILLING CENTERS

You increase your insight into your life when you realize that everything you do or feel has a greater or lesser bearing on each of the first five Centers. For example, when you are eating, you are experiencing the food predominantly from the Sensation Center as you enjoy the taste. However, eating has aspects that involve the Security Center, for food can serve as an emotional crutch to make you feel secure. And, of course, the basic nutritional value in the food is connected with your security. Or your food can be experienced from the Power Center by pontificating to others as to what foods they really should be eating to become holy. Your food can be enjoyed from the Love Center as a way of accepting and loving new tastes. Or your food can be appreciated from the point of view of the Cornucopia Center as a further confirmation that you live in a beautiful world that gives you everything you need in order to live in higher consciousness. As you grow, you will begin to experience your food from any combination of the five Centers—*or all of them.*

In each of the five preceding Centers, you will find that you are continually judging yourself. In greater or lesser degree, you are comparing your thoughts and actions with a Center of Consciousness to determine whether you are meeting the standards of the Center. Each Center presents you with something to do: (1) achieving security, (2) experiencing sensations, (3) developing power, (4) attaining the ability to love and accept everyone and everything unconditionally no matter what happens, and (5) experiencing the friendliness and perfection of everything around you.

Even though you are not supposed to be driving yourself, you may constantly be wondering whether you are really progressing rapidly. You may be saying inwardly, "Is Bob growing faster than I?" "What's holding me back? I thought my consciousness was at the Love Center and I just became aware of power aspects of our relationship." "Did I just blow it?" "Does it help to keep a record of how many minutes a day I am on each of the Centers?" "Should I allow myself one month to get rid of most of the thoughts of the lower three Centers?"

You will go through phases in which you are addicted to the Love Center and the Cornucopia Center. You may become impatient because you thought you were loving unconditionally—and you find something that you could not emotionally accept. Then you may get the feeling, "I've just got to rush this through and then I can relax again and stop manipulating the people and things around me. I can really begin flowing for the rest of my life when I work through this problem."

Although your growth toward higher consciousness is associated with unconditionally accepting yourself and others, you will find that you experience each of the first five levels of consciousness as a standard by which you measure yourself. And isn't this an addiction? Each of these five Centers of Consciousness may be regarded as chains that keep you vulnerable to fear, resentment, anger, anxiety, worry, etc. Even when your consciousness resides most of the time in the Cornucopia Center, it is still chained—although it may be regarded as a light chain of fine gold.

THE SIXTH CENTER OF CONSCIOUSNESS— THE CONSCIOUS-AWARENESS CENTER

The way to become free of these chains is to let your consciousness reside in your Conscious-awareness Center. This is a peaceful place that is experienced from deep inside where you just witness your drama in all of the other five Centers. *In this Center you do not judge or evaluate in any way.* You just witness yourself, "There he is in the unconditional Love Center. He just had a thought that he cannot really be loving when Mary gets mad at him. He's putting himself down because he cannot yet experience everything as a form of love."

From the detached Conscious-awareness Center, you just watch yourself performing in all of the other five Centers. You don't pat yourself on the back or criticize yourself in any way. You blissfully enjoy the show. You impartially witness yourself. You let your drama be anything—and everything.

You use the Conscious-awareness Center as a meta-center from which you get free from your preoccupation with the preceding five Centers of Consciousness—for all the five Centers bind you in one way or another by creating a special version of what's happening. You break through all chains when you experience every moment of your life from that deep, calm place inside you where you observe everything—and accept everything.

The Conscious-awareness Center gives you a space between you and the surrounding world. From this Center you are no longer vulnerable to ups and downs. At last you are free—nothing can disturb you or bring you down even though your body and mind may be going through various types of drama. You still have to "chop wood and carry water" regardless of the Center of Consciousness you are on. You will still want to play an active part in the world around you. You will still be learning various things, interacting with people, and doing your part in building a more beautiful world by living a conscious life. *But* YOU *will not be doing it.* It will only be your body and mind that are involved in these daily dramas of working, playing, feeling, doing, etc. Your Conscious-awareness will be watching it all as a magic show from a beautiful place deep inside you where everything is peaceful—all the time. Even if your body and mind go through the manifestations of anger or jealousy, you are aware that you are only playing out one of your addictive roles in your dramatic repertory. For you are just silently witnessing your body and mind picking up the cues and saying your lines as others recite their lines in the daily drama of life.

When you live in the Sixth Center of Consciousness you will experience yourself as an actor on the great stage of life. Each day you act out the lines that are dictated by the programming of your biocomputer. And you know that the cues others pick up and their responses to them are a function of the Centers of Consciousness that they are experiencing at the now moment in their journey toward awakening.

Each of us creates a world that is generated by the Centers of Consciousness that we are using in today's script of the cosmic play. Central casting has furnished various people who are dressed up as actors for the purpose of helping you in your consciousness growth. But your higher consciousness is out in the "audience" watching your body and mind interact with other bodies and minds on stage. And you view everything you do and say as part of your growth toward freedom from your addictive traps.

Your addictive programs that activate your ego and your rational mind constantly keep you from realizing who you really are. The way to tell "what you think you are" or "who you think you are" is to notice carefully what your ego is guarding. What are the "fronts" or social images that you are now in the process of living out? What things trigger anger, fear, jealousy, or grief? What "somebody" does your rational mind defend? Whatever dance you are now doing and *backing up with your ego represents who you now think you are*. All of this programming keeps you vulnerable and insecure.

What images do you have of yourself? What kind of impression do you want to make on others? Do you project yourself as an achieving person, a competent person, a "help-poor-me" person, someone that the world takes advantage of, a good mother, a good father, a good businessman or businesswoman, a "drop-out," one who is versed in various knowledge games, an artistic person, or a real expert in the sex games? Or perhaps your ego is guarding your image of being very perceptive of the foibles of our civilization and definitely above it all. Perhaps you have some hobbies and you guard your image as a guitar player, motorcyclist, surfer, painter, poet, singer, or whatever. Or it may be that you are through with these mundane projections of your self image. Perhaps your ego is now guarding a "pure" you as a climber of the mystical spiritual mountain. Do you get upset when someone points out that your way is not the only way or not the best way for him or her? What are the various games into which your ego is directing your energy and consciousness at this time in your life?

When you clearly see your various activities, games, and personal boundaries as a drama that your ego is now trying to guard and enhance, you will understand who you now think you are. . . . But you are not any of this "stuff." All of this stuff is simply a dance that you are going through to discover the conscious being that you really are. If you were to write a list of all the activities, attributes, personality characteristics, and personal boundaries that your ego is now defending, you will find that many of them were not on the list ten years ago. And if you grow toward higher consciousness, most of them will not be on the list ten years from now. As you increase in consciousness, you see with perspective the way you are busily engaged in a mechanical playing-out of the roles in which you have programmed yourself.

All of these things that your ego is busy defending act as a series of boxes that keep you trapped. Every box suffocates and is your ever-present source of vulnerability on the roller-coaster of pleasure and pain. Most of the addictive models you are now guarding represent patterns of personality that are a function of the time and place where you were born and grew up. If you had been born in a different social group, your ego would be busily engaged in guarding a different set of roles.

The world is here for us to enjoy, but we can totally enjoy it only when we are free from identifying with the roles we play in the drama of life. The only way to continuously enjoy a game of chess or checkers is to avoid taking it so seriously that you get emotionally caught up in either winning or losing. Human beings (with their big rational minds) enjoy solving problems. But we tend to take these problems with such seriousness (perhaps due to our prestige addictions) that we kill the aliveness and fun of our here-and-now life situation. We need a way to discriminate between what we essentially are and the motivational models that generate our behavior.

To get free of our identification with the social games in which we are now trapped, we must clearly see the games for what they are. It can be helpful to experience a book such as Ruth Benedict's *Patterns of Culture*. When we see the mores of our tribe from the perspective of comparative anthropology, it helps us liberate ourselves from our cultural traps. When we really see the economic and social folkways of our in-group with insight, how can our egos continue to get away with demanding so much that we really don't need in order to be happy? How can we take so seriously the many prestige games in which we are now engaged? How can our pride keep us imprisoned in the meaningless "loss or gain" and "fame or shame" games that we previously thought were necessary to make our lives work?

A conscious being does not reject either his individual games or society's games—he just plays them as games. If our group says, "Let's play the game of keeping the sexual parts of our body covered when we walk down Main Street," it is accepted as a part of the here-and-now games of life. If a conscious being is in a place where the group says, "Here is a beach or a hot springs where nude bathing takes place," an individual without addictions in this area can also flow with what is here and now. Except where individuals are being harmed, conscious people flow with the activities and feelings of the group. They are magnificently flexible, and they are comfortable with whatever dance the social orchestra may be playing. They are equally comfortable in trying to change the dance—for they usually find ways to work toward change from an "us" space. Their consciousness, love, insight, and flexibility give us messages that help us spring free from the social rigidities that we thought were "natural."

So we gradually learn that we are not these personalities that our egos are defending so valiantly. If we are not our personalities, this collection of motivations that we have picked up from our society, just what—or who—are we? Many of us identify our selves with our bodies—this changing structure of bones, muscles, and other organs enclosed by our skin. When our bodies are not well or are transmitting a sensation of pain to our biocomputer, our egos tend to focus attention on the pain so that we identify completely with the pain. As we grow into higher consciousness, we increasingly realize that we are not the bodies we live in. Our bodies are just temples that are the homes of our consciousness.

Once you stop identifying with your various social roles and your body, you will probably say, "Aha! My essence is my rational mind." For isn't this the essence of being human? This is the part of your biocomputer that has the ability to use language, to analyze, to calculate, to produce thoughts and images, to sort out sensations, to store them away in memory and to retrieve them, to use symbols, to compare beliefs and assumptions, etc. Didn't Aristotle define man as a rational animal? But here again, your rational mind is not *your essence*. Your intellect or rational mind is a magnificent "sixth sense" that can help you in your journey to higher consciousness if you know how to use it properly. Or it can keep you helplessly trapped in the lower three Centers of Consciousness by slavishly cooperating with your ego to form rigid, logical defenses that maintain whatever programming you are now stuck with. So you let this one go too. . . .

You are now getting it narrowed down. If you are not your social roles, your body, or your rational mind, just what is left? Are you your senses—the various gates through which visual, auditory, tactile, taste, and olfactory data are received? Or are you your emotions—those feeling tones that you expend so much energy in either getting or avoiding? Are you your programming—the collections of desires, motivations, expectations, and demands on which your ego focuses most of your attention and energy? Or are you your ego—that "master controller" that is such an absolute dictator when you are trapped in the lower three Centers of Consciousness? Fortunately, the essential you is none of these, either. And so we continue the search for "you." Could it be that the search for your essence is clouded by your ego-backed programming that wants you to be "somebody"? Does your name, your memory, and your rational mind combine to give you the illusion that you are a specific entity that should make a splash as you pass through the world of people and things?

At this point you may have the feeling, "There's nothing left of me." But your essence is something which you may experience to help you grow into higher consciousness. In the Living Love Way, we define your essence as your *Conscious-awareness.* To understand what we mean by Conscious-awareness, look straight ahead of you and notice for a minute the images that are being transmitted through your eyes. Then close your eyes. Do it now before reading on. . . .

The visual sensations disappeared—but your Conscious-awareness remained. Behind all of your thoughts, sensations, and images, your Conscious-awareness is always there. Most of the time we keep it smothered under a ceaseless Niagara of words, activities, thoughts, and sensations which keep our minds analyzing, calculating, symbolizing, talking, remembering, futuring, and pasting.

The experiment above demonstrates that your visual field and your Conscious-awareness are not the same. Let's go further. Close your eyes. Do it now for one minute before reading on. . . .

What were you aware of? When you shut off the visual input to your biocomputer, you probably became aware of sounds. But sounds are not your Conscious-awareness. Suppose you go to a completely dark, quiet place. With the visual and sound inputs quiet, you may now begin to tune in to your body on deeper and deeper levels. You can experience bodily sensations that have previously been up-staged by the more dominating happenings of your five senses and the stimulation of your ideas, thoughts, and words. You only experience your essence fully when you have quieted your emotion-backed drama and the torrent of addictive stuff churned out by your rational mind.

In other words, you are *the awareness of your consciousness!* You might wish to visualize a television screen in the middle of your head where all of your thoughts, images, and emotions are projected. It's all there in color—including sights, sounds, words, and thought. It's all going by on this imaginary television screen in the middle of your head. But you are not the television screen. You are not the images or stuff on the screen. *You are that which is conscious of being aware of all of the stuff which is running on the screen.* You are simply the watcher of the stuff on the screen. As Ram Dass puts it, "Observe your scene from a quiet corner of your mind in which there is nothing to do but 'see.'" You are the conciousness that just "sees" what is happening on the screen. Your essence is *pure Conscious-awareness.*

As the watcher of the screen, you are perfect. The screen may be projecting a horrendous movie that is showing all kinds of pain and suffering—on the screen. Or the screen may reflect a happy movie that shows a beautiful sunset, a delightful sexual experience, or an enjoyable meal. But the essential you is the pure awareness that just watches the stuff go by on the screen of your life. *Behind what you think you are*—YOU ARE!

The essential you is perfect, has always been perfect, and always will be perfect! There is nothing you can do to alter the perfection of the essential you. *And this perfection does not need to be guarded with* ego. When you realize who or what you really are, your ego can relax and you can really enjoy your life. For nothing poses either a threat or an "absolute necessity" to you any longer. You can truly enjoy being the *essential you*—and only then can you totally and continuously enjoy the unfolding drama that your life brings you.

As you begin to experience yourself as the watcher of the drama from the Sixth Center of Consciousness, you no longer labor under the illusion that your intellectual effort, will, and frantic paranoid watchfulness are necessary to keep the world operating properly. Instead you experience the power, the deep peace, and the exquisite beauty of letting your energy harmonize with the energies around you. You realize that by tuning in to the Ocean of loving energy around you, you can have far more security, enjoyable sensations, effectiveness, and love than you ever need in order to live a continuously beautiful life. And as you learn to identify the essential you with your Conscious-awareness (instead of with the social and individual stuff that your ego has backed up in the past) you deeply and continuously enjoy both the drama of your life and the perfect being that you naturally are.

THE SEVENTH CENTER OF CONSCIOUSNESS—THE COSMIC CONSCIOUSNESS CENTER

You will observe that your growth towards the highest Centers of Consciousness may fall naturally into three phases:

1. *As your consciousness begins* to dwell more and more in the Love Center and Cornucopia Center, you will begin to develop a multi-centered perception that will enable you to see all of your thoughts and actions from each of the first five Centers.
2. *Continuing this multi-centered awareness,* you learn to witness yourself on the detached Conscious-awareness Center (the Sixth Center). At this level, there is no longer a feeling of lower or higher consciousness—it is all the same from the Conscious-awareness Center. And then,
3. *You go behind the Conscious-awareness Center* to the selfless, unitive space of the Cosmic Consciousness Center.

The Sixth Center of Consciousness is characterized by being aware of yourself. There is your essence—your Conscious-awareness—and there is the daily drama of your body, your senses, and your rational mind. You see all of your drama with insight and perspective. Although this is a peaceful, beautiful Center of Consciousness, there is still duality. There is still a fine line of separation between you and the world.

On the seventh level of consciousness, one is catapulted from *self-awareness* into *pure awareness.* In other words, one is no longer witnessing oneself. The body, mind, senses, and Conscious-awareness are not separated. In this Center of Consciousness, one does not *experience* security, sensations, power, love, and Cornucopia—one *is* security, sensations, power, love, and the fullness of life. The highest state of consciousness is attained by reprogramming what is called the "self." One's thought activity is calmed. The direction of perception has shifted from subject-object manipulation, through a phase of loving acceptance, *to a unity with everything in the environment.*

To understand this distinction between experiencing something and being something, consider what happens when you have an intense sexual climax. Up until the time of orgasm, you have been experiencing the sexual sensations such as increasing warmth, pressure, and stimulation of your sexual organs. You are experiencing sex. But at the moment of sexual climax you are no longer the experiencer. You may no longer be conscious of *yourself* enjoying sexual happenings. During the moments of an intense orgasm, *you are the experience.* At that moment you may feel a total oneness with your sexual partner—for there is no longer the experience of you as a separate consciousness.

At the Cosmic Consciousness level, one can function with enormous effectiveness because the screens that limit one's receptiveness have been eliminated. One is now tuned to the finer nuances of the surrounding world. One is open to the broad spectrum of all of the finer cues that the world has been sending all the time—but which were previously not picked up by a consciousness occupied by security, sensation, and power on the lower levels, and love, Cornucopia, and witnessing on the intermediate levels.

And now at the end of one's journey to higher consciousness, one has become a god-like being. One has truly achieved one's birthright. As a fully conscious being, one is optimally perceptive, optimally wise, and optimally effective. Because one has transcended all personal boundaries, and experiences no separation from anyone or anything in the world, serving "others" is the only thing to do in life. For there are no "others." Everything is experienced from an "us" space.

Perhaps a word of advice may be helpful here. The Seventh Center is extremely difficult to attain. Out of the four billion people in this world, there may only be about a hundred people who are consistently in that Center. Achieving it usually requires a detached life style and a long period of intense consciousness growth practice. Even preferences must be eliminated to reach this Center. The author of this book generates his experience of life using the Fourth, Fifth, and Sixth Centers and enjoys life continuously. This does not mean he is a hundred per cent free of addictions, but he often goes many weeks without any separating emotional feelings.

When you have eliminated about ninety-nine per cent of your addictive programming, the remaining amount will probably be very subtle and will not interfere with happiness. When you have done the inner work required to get to this level of effectiveness, you know exactly which Pathway or Method to use whenever you experience the beginning of an addictive sequence. Within seconds or minutes you work through whatever security, sensation, or power addiction you are triggering and then you are right back at the Love or Cornucopia Center again. These Centers are totally adequate to enable you to live a happy, fulfilled, wise, effective, and enjoyable life. It is worthwhile knowing about the Cosmic Consciousness Center, but do not let it become another addiction. If you work hard to use the Fourth, Fifth, or Sixth Centers of Consciousness in processing and interpreting your own energies and the energies of the world around you, you will experience a deep peace and enjoyment within your heart that is wholly enough.

13
five methods for working on yourself

The Living Love Way to Higher Consciousness offers you Five Methods that you can use in working on yourself. These Methods have been chosen for busy people who are deeply involved in various dramas of life. They do not detach you from your daily routines. The Living Love Methods can be used while you are engaged in running a business, making love, cleaning the house, or watching a movie. These Methods *take you into your life situations* and require you to view the people and things around you as your teachers. *But you are really your master teacher all the time.*

When you use these Five Methods continuously in your moment-to-moment daily life, you will find a turned-on satisfaction in your daily stream of consciousness. You will experience a liberation that you have always wanted, but have not been able to find in life before. You will find true freedom from the computer-like programming that separates and alienates you from the loving being you naturally are.

Here are the Five Methods:

METHOD NO. 1

Memorize the Twelve Pathways and use them to guide you through your daily life situations.

When you learn to use them, you will find that the Twelve Pathways furnish you with the complete solution to every emotional problem in your life. But to benefit maximally from them, you must *intuitively* use them on the deepest levels of awareness. Once you have them memorized, say them before getting up in the morning and before going to sleep at night. This may increase your probability of realizing the Fourth Center of Consciousness in a year or two instead of many years or even decades.

Whenever you feel worried, angry, jealous, fearful, anxious, or any other uncomfortable emotional feeling, *life is giving you a message.* It is *always* telling you that you are not following the Twelve Pathways. Your next step is to find the ones that you are not using and let them show you what to do to feel beautiful again.

Stop churning over the usual questions that you ask yourself (which have not helped you find solutions). If these usual ways of talking to yourself were effective, you would be happy, peaceful, serene, and loving—here and now. Instead of using your past way of talking to yourself, just keep going over the Twelve Pathways. Remember that their purpose is to keep you centered, tuned in, conscious, and loving. They are not designed to help you manipulate the people and things around you to make them fit your inside addictions. The Twelve Pathways will help you reprogram your mind so that ALL of your addictions become preferences—and then you can live peacefully. The more you are uptight, the more important it is for you to stop worrying about the outside condition that you feel "makes you upset." Instead, concentrate on the inner addictions or expectations with which you hassle yourself.

The Twelve Pathways will show you what it means to be truly alive. You will look back to your present state of consciousness and realize that you have been far more dead than alive. Everything you need will come to you in a seemingly miraculous fashion as you live with these Pathways. The peace, love, and effectiveness that you have always wanted will be yours.

METHOD NO. 2

Be aware at all times of which Center of Consciousness you are experiencing.

You will discover that working on your consciousness is the most fulfilling thing you can do in your life. Whether you are driving a car, reading a book, or even caught in an addictive argument with someone, you can always add to the beauty of your outside drama if you are constantly aware of what Center of Consciousness you are using.

Everything you do has aspects on all levels of consciousness. We can enjoy life *on all levels*—and not just be hung up on the lower three Centers. For example, if you are making love, you can be aware of security aspects (the Security Center), or you can just enjoy the groovy feelings (the Sensation Center), or you can be conscious of the submission or control aspects (the Power Center). You can be aware of love-making as an act of pure acceptance of another and an experience of unconditional love (the Love Center). The act of love-making is another manifestation of the way the world offers you everything you need (the Cornucopia Center). Or you can watch the entire drama from your Center of Centers (the Conscious-awareness Center).

As you constantly uplevel the Center of Consciousness that you are experiencing, you will find that each time you go up one Center of Consciousness, you interact with more and more people. You will also liberate more and more energy. For example, if you are totally preoccupied with security, you will not have much energy for seeking sensations and power. And you cannot feel close to people when your consciousness is concerned solely with your security. On this level people are objects to be manipulated. You find increasing involvement with people and increasing energy as you uplevel to the Sensation Center, the Power Center, and then to the Love Center and the Cornucopia Center. *Each Center generates more energy and lets you relate to more people than the previous Center.* Each Center opens the door to an increased enrichment of your life.

Your awareness of which Center of Consciousness you are experiencing and your use of the Twelve Pathways to continually guide you are the Living Love Way to *meditate*. And you do this all the time in your busy life so that *your entire life becomes meditation.* In the Living Love Way, meditation is not a holy ritual to be performed once or twice a day. It is a method for consistently seeing things clearly and consciously—here and now.

METHOD NO. 3

Link the suffering with the addiction to get the intellectual and emotional insight that it is your addictive demand that is causing your suffering.

To tune in to the enormous *effectiveness* of the Living Love Way, it is essential that you become increasingly conscious of each of your addictions and **the way it generates a series of events that make you suffer.** It is important that you notice how each addiction involves your ego and your rational mind—which, instead of letting go of the addiction, begins to churn out a "rational" solution which triggers another round of problems in your life.

Changes leading to happiness come most rapidly when you can fully engage both your ego and rational mind (two of your most powerful faculties) in the game of helping you eliminate each addiction. Many addictions will rapidly melt away as soon as you consciously experience that the suffering they cause is actually due to the addiction. Some of the deeper addictions that were programmed into your biocomputer with pain during the first two or three years of your life require more inner work and more "living through" to fully experience the extensive ramifications of the pattern of suffering they are bringing into your life. The key to the Third Method is *to consciously connect all of the suffering in your life with the addictive, emotion-backed models and expectations that you keep telling yourself you must have to be happy.*

This Method is so basic and fundamental that it is difficult to overstate its importance. If you are extremely upset and you don't remember the Pathways, the Seven Centers of Consciousness, or any other Method, this Third Method (that calls for pinpointing the addiction and connecting it with the unhappiness and suffering in your life) should be able to help you become conscious again! Resolve now that you will never again let your ego and rational mind try to convince you that the outside world is doing it to you—that others are the cause of your suffering. Whenever you lay the responsibility for your emotional feelings on the people and things around you, you perpetuate your entrapment in your security, sensation, and power programming. To break loose from these lower consciousness traps, you must always take full responsibility for what you are experiencing and get to work as quickly as possible on the addiction that causes you to reject emotionally what people are doing or saying.

By taking full responsibility, you give your ego and rational mind an entirely different direction in which to operate. They begin to work on helping you to reprogram instead of egging you on to manipulate and fight the people in your life. *This changed direction of regard from the outside world to your own inner programming is the key to benefiting from this unusually rapid Method of consciousness growth.* If you become an expert at pinpointing the addiction that you are using to trigger your fear, anger, grief, resentment, or jealousy, within several months you may be able to enjoy the Fourth Center of Consciousness much of the time. Your energy, perceptiveness and love will soar to create a new "you."

See yourself go through the following four steps in your process of liberation:

TO BE FREE

1. **Explore the suffering.**
2. **Pinpoint the addictive demand.**
3. **Reprogram the addictive demand.**
4. **Experience the freedom.**

To become competent in applying the Third Method, you should develop your own technique for becoming aware of which addiction is causing you to feel alienated from the here and now in your life. You may wish to ask yourself such questions as: "What is happening right now?" (In answering this do not use your rational mind or your ego to justify, intellectualize, or interpret. Just give the facts of what is happening, such as who, what, when, where, and how.) "What specific emotion am I experiencing?" (In answering this *tell what you feel—not what you think.* Words that describe emotional feelings are: anxious, harried, bored, lonely, shy, irritable, annoyed, frustrated, confused, sad, depressed, disappointed, worried, afraid, resentful, hostile, angry, jealous, grief-filled, guilty, tense, nervous, embarrassed, etc.) "What am I telling myself right now?" "What pains or tensions are being evoked in my body at this moment?" "What do my posture and face look like?" "What is the dance that my rational mind is doing to prove me right and everybody else wrong?" "What do I want to change in the outside world instead of doing the inner work of changing my own response to it?" "What sort of phony front is my ego trying to maintain?" "What past events were particularly painful so as to give my biocomputer this programming that makes me upset when a similar event happens?" "Have I suffered enough?" "Do I really want to be free from this automatic response whenever the here and now of my life checks me out?" "Exactly what am I rejecting in the here and now?" "What am I rejecting about myself?" "What threat does this person or situation represent to me?" "What is the *worst* that could happen?" "Could I accept this and still be happy?" "What am I defending?" "What am I hiding?" "What is it about me that I think people can't love?" "What do I imagine the other person is thinking?" "What mask am I wearing?" "What dances are my pride and my prestige making me perform?" "What am I demanding in order to feel happy and enough? Of myself? Of others? Of the outside world?" "What is the model I have of the way I should be, must be, or have to be?" "What is the model of the way I should be treated?" "What are the specific details of the model that I have of the way the world should be in order for me to be accepting, loving, and flowing?" "What Center of Consciousness am I operating out of?" "If a magic genie were to appear at this moment, and this genie had the power to alter the situation exactly as I instruct, what request would I make of this genie?"

Once you have pinpointed the addiction, your next step is to reprogram it into a preference. When you reprogram, you use your will and determination to give clear, firm operating instructions to your biocomputer. You tell it that you want it to function in a different way in processing incoming data in the future. This means that with intensity and conviction, you put a new operating instruction into your mind. *Reprogramming works most effectively if you repeat the reprogramming instruction many, many, many times.* The next chapter, which deals with Consciousness Focusing, gives you additional information on how to give a "knock-out punch" to your heavier addictions.

Always remember that the key to using the Third Method is to look deeply within yourself to find the emotion-backed demand that you are using to upset yourself. It's this simple. Just become more consciously conscious of the cause-effect relationship between your addictions and the resulting unhappiness, and you will be on the escalator that can take you directly to the Fourth Center of Consciousness.

METHOD NO. 4
Use the Catalyst ALL WAYS US LIVING LOVE as a tool for cognitive centering.

Your growth into higher consciousness can be more rapid if you keep a Catalyst going in your mind as a foreground figure against which all of your sensations, feelings, and thoughts are the background. This constant repetition helps you to calm your mind, to increase your powers of concentration, to broaden your perceptions, to permit your intuitive wisdom to emerge, to free you from your addictions, and to keep you feeling great.

The Catalyst ALL WAYS US LIVING LOVE can be slowly and silently repeated to enable you to continuously tune in to that part of you that does not see others as *him, her,* or *them*—but always *us.* Oneness is yours when you feel everyone as *only us*—when you see things through the eyes of others and feel things within their psychic space as though it were your own.

After you have accumulated several hours of experience with

the Catalyst, you will probably feel its vibrations and implications on deeper and deeper levels. Since only one thing can receive your full attention at a time, this centering technique can crowd out negative thoughts and feelings and replace them with the vibrations of Living Love. This enables you to control your racing mind-stuff whenever you wish.

A repeated phrase constantly recaptures your attention. The Catalyst ALL WAYS US LIVING LOVE may be used to change your mood in a positive way. When you are disturbed or have an upsetting experience, you can repeat this phrase over and over until you feel calm and centered. Through consistent practice, it will develop increasingly greater effectiveness.

This tool for cognitive centering can be most effective if you:

1. *Consecutively emphasize* each of the words as follows: "ALL Ways Us Living Love," "All WAYS Us Living Love," "All Ways US Living Love," etc.

2. If you say it aloud, open up your mouth and throat when you say the word "ALL." Feel it resonate in your heart. Let the whole world flow into your openness. If you say it silently, feel this openness.

3. *Say or sing* each word lovingly and caressingly. Singing is usually more effective in calming the mind than just speaking, for it leaves little or no space on the screen of your consciousness for random thoughts.

4. *Almost from the first time* you use it, the Catalyst may be so effective at bringing peace and quietness to your mind that it may be best not to drive your car or operate dangerous machinery until you have gained experience in using it. With experience you will be able to "adjust" your use of it so that you will have the energy and perceptiveness for here-and-now activities without becoming inattentive.

5. *One who is seriously working* on consciousness growth may wish to use the Catalyst for thirty minutes a day for at least one month in order to become proficient in its use. It then becomes an effective consciousness tool that is available when needed. At times of great stress, one may find it useful to use it over and over continuously throughout the day.

To increase your perceptiveness of people, you may wish to use the Catalyst as you look into their faces. This helps you get behind your games and their games to the place where we are just loving beings. You may wish to avoid eye-to-eye contact as this can involve ego ("I can look at you more penetratingly than you can look at me"). Instead find a small patch of light at the bridge of the nose between the eyes that is created by most lighting conditions. With your eyes fixed on this spot, experience the many changes in the face that are perceived as you run the Catalyst.

METHOD NO. 5
Consciousness Focusing.

One of the most powerful of the Living Love Methods is the technique of Consciousness Focusing. This Method is explained in detail in the next two chapters.

14 CONSCIOUSNESS FOCUSING

Consciousness Focusing is one of the most powerful Methods for reprogramming strong addictions. When used effectively, a lifetime addiction can sometimes be wiped out of one's emotional programming in a surprisingly short time. The greater the opportunity that something offers us for security, pleasurable sensations, or power, the more we will have developed addictive programming that exposes us to disappointment and suffering. Consciousness Focusing helps us reprogram these strong addictions that make us expend so much futile energy in guarding them and living them out in our daily dance.

Consciousness Focusing helps us to use our present life situations to grow maximally. To use this new Method, we go forward in life rather than retreat from it. For example, if your marriage relationship is uncomfortable to you or if you are upsetting yourself in your business affairs, you can use this effective technique to grow much more rapidly than if you did not have such heavy life problems.

Consciousness Focusing is based on the fact that your emotional programming is established by whatever you tell yourself with strong feelings when you are in pain and suffering. Actually, you've been using Consciousness Focusing all of your life. Perhaps when you were a young child you stuck your finger into a light bulb socket and received an electric shock. You instantly withdrew your finger in pain, and told yourself that the light bulb socket was the cause of the pain. That may have been the last time you ever did that because your biocomputer strongly programmed an instruction, "I will not put my finger in light bulb sockets because it hurts." From then on in your life, whenever your finger even got near the inside of a light bulb socket, a "red flag" went up in you to make sure you didn't get shocked again.

When you are peaceful and calm, you have the best opportunity to reprogram your rational mind—but not your emotion-backed addictions. For example, you can study a book or listen to a lecture most effectively when you are calm. Your biocomputer will not handle the lecture or book very well when you are upset because your addictions have the ability to dominate and override other processes in your biocomputer. But *when you are emotionally upset,* you then have a superlative opportunity to reprogram your addictions by using the Consciousness Focusing Method. Thus every time you feel fearful, jealous, anxious, or angry, your life is giving you a golden opportunity to use this method to liberate yourself from an addiction.

Consciousness Focusing can be used at any time to work on an addiction. However, it is most effective in getting rid of a deeper level security, sensation, or power addiction when, in the past few weeks, you (1) have applied the Pathways, (2) are aware of what Center of Consciousness you were using to make yourself upset, and (3) have used the Third Method to connect the addiction with the suffering that you are feeling.

You may use Consciousness Focusing to reprogram a heavy addiction *when you want freedom from the addiction more intensely than you want a change in the external world.* For example, after a five-month period of repeatedly experiencing jealousy, I wanted freedom from the addiction that triggered the separating emotion of jealousy more than I wanted to control the woman I was with. At that point, in about 90 minutes of Consciousness Focusing, I apparently reprogrammed the addictions which trigger jealousy for the rest of my life.* Usually, however, repeated reprogramming sessions are necessary.

* A description of this experience is available in a cassette entitled *My Triumph Over Jealousy* which can be obtained from Ken Keyes College Bookroom, 790 Commercial Ave., Coos Bay, OR 97420. Cost is $6.95 plus $1.50 for postage and handling.

Here's the way to use the Method of Consciousness Focusing:

Step 1. EXPLORE THE SUFFERING

First, review *the bare facts* of the incident that triggered your fear, anger, jealousy, or other disturbing feelings. Then let yourself experience the suffering that you are creating inside of you. Notice how your body feels—your head, your shoulders, your heart, your stomach, your legs, your back, your arms, and your insides. Describe to yourself in simple words *what you are feeling.* Use words such as afraid, anxious, depressed, jealous, angry, resentful, irritated, etc. Don't think about it or give reasons—just observe what you are feeling and give one word descriptions that refer to feeling states.

Step 2. PINPOINT THE ADDICTION

Now pinpoint the addiction (or addictions) that are responsible for your suffering in the situation you outlined in Step 1 above. Clearly formulate the exact addictive demands that you are making. You may wish to review the Third Method explained in the previous chapter which tells how to formulate the addiction. To get rid of suffering, you must first know the immediate cause. The cause of the suffering will always be an emotion-backed program in your head. This addictive programming must always be present as an intervening variable between the chain of events in the outside world and your uptightness and unhappiness. If you did not have this addictive demand, the outside events would be powerless to trigger what you are now experiencing. It works this way:

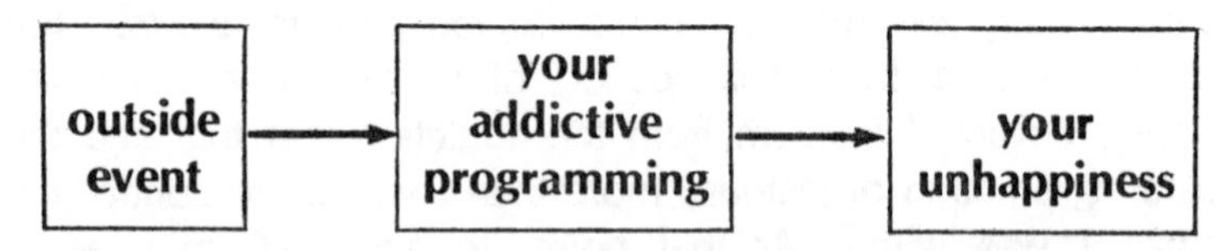

If you remove the middle factor, there is no way the outside event can make you generate an unhappy experience. Your ego and rational mind have been blaming the left hand box (the outside event) for your suffering. You are now training your nervous system to take responsibility for your experience. You'll have to deeply convince your rational mind that your addictive demands are the immediate cause of your suffering. Be very specific in pinpointing the demand.

Exactly what do you want in that situation? What would you like to change in that situation? Tune in to your feelings and check to make sure you feel that you've pinpointed the demand which is causing your suffering.

Step 3. SELECT YOUR REPROGRAMMING PHRASES

First look back at all the past suffering you have brought to yourself in similar situations. Usually your ego and rational mind blamed others for your unhappiness. This kept you from seeing that it is your own addictions that have created the problems in your life. Look at the long chain of similar events in your past. Take full responsibility for the fact that you were doing it to yourself. Now look beyond the present into the future. How many years do you probably have to live? How long do you want to continue to make yourself unhappy over this sort of thing? **Have you really had enough unhappiness and feelings of alienation, pain, and separateness from this addictive demand?** Proceed when you are sure.

Now select a reprogramming instruction that you want to forcefully put into your biocomputer. *This will be a direct command to your biocomputer.* Experience has shown that this command can either be in a negative form such as, "I don't have to be jealous when my lover is with someone else" or a positive form such as "I am enough." Your marvelous biocomputer is excellent at handling instructions both to do something or not to do something. Choose a reprogramming phrase that is short, pithy, and that feels good when you say it rapidly with intensity behind it. Start out with a reprogramming phrase that directly refers to the situation covered in Step 1 above. Thus, "I don't need to feel worthless when Sue rejects me" is a specific level to start with. Then you can go on to more general programmings like, "It is really harmless to be rejected!" "I don't have to get upset when I'm rejected!" "You win some and you lose some!" *Don't start reprogramming until you are completely fed up with the addictive demand.* When you see clearly that it is your addiction that is immediately causing your suffering and not the situation in itself, and when you see how unnecessary it is to make the demands you have been making, then you are ready to start reprogramming. If you still feel you would rather satisfy your addictions than get rid of them, you are not ready to reprogram. In that case, use the other methods to gain insights. Link the suffering with the addiction, continually looking at the suffering which that addiction creates in your life and seeing how it is just your addictive programming which creates the suffering—not the outside world. Remind yourself that negative, separating emotions never help you to get what you really want; they only work against you.

Step 4. FOCUS YOUR CONSCIOUSNESS ON REPROGRAMMING

Now tense your body all over to build up tension in your autonomic nervous system *and thus add to your readiness to modify your emotional programming.* You will find that a position kneeling on the floor with your head down near your knees will facilitate this method. (It does not need to be done in that position, however.) With maximum determination to get rid of the addiction that is causing your suffering, forcefully repeat one or more reprogramming phrases you have selected. Do it over and over and over again. It may help to yell or cry when you repeat these phrases. But it's your determination and will to be free of the addiction that really accomplishes the reprogramming—not the noise. Clench your fists or beat on the floor as you say the reprogramming phrase. Tighten your arm or leg muscles, or do anything else that feels good to you while you repeatedly hammer your reprogramming phrase into the deepest parts of your biocomputer. If you are yelling during Consciousness Focusing, you can use a pillow or a small plastic waste basket (head size!) with a sponge in it to reduce the noise. The wastebasket both amplifies the sound in your ears and helps you keep your neighbors happier by greatly cutting down on the outside sound.

Keep focusing your reprogramming phrases into your biocomputer by forcefully repeating them over and over again with intense determination to be free. If your biocomputer is ready to let go of the old programming that is causing your suffering, the emotional charge that you experience as you repeat these phrases will become less and less. You will begin to develop a feeling of buoyancy and freedom. Consciousness Focusing feels great when done correctly. Constantly keep in mind that this procedure for Consciousness Focusing is effective to the degree that you have thoroughly linked your suffering with a specific addictive programming that your ego and rational mind have been guarding and defending. *Consciousness Focusing works to the degree that you really desire freedom from the addiction.* If part of you still really wants the outside world to change in order for you to be happy, your attempts at Consciousness Focusing will be only partially effective. You can't fool your biocomputer into reprogramming *unless you really mean it and want it.*

When you experience an addiction, if possible use Consciousness Focusing immediately. It always works best when you use the *initial emotional surge* that makes you feel afraid, angry, jealous, or resentful. If you are not ready to do Consciousness Focusing, use one of the other methods so that you can gain the insights which will enable you to drop the addiction. If your emotions cool out, it will be more difficult to generate the emotional energy. But using Consciousness Focusing at a later time can still be very effective. It always helps in some degree in chipping away part of our heavier rock-like addictions.

If you get in touch with an addiction when you are in an elevator, or seated in the middle of a big auditorium, it obviously will not be practical for you to immediately crouch down on the floor and engage in vigorous verbal reprogramming. In public situations, you can develop the ability to step up your determination, and just silently use the reprogramming phrases you have selected.

The above four steps are basic procedures for Consciousness Focusing.* There are, however, a number of background techniques that will help you improve your skill in Consciousness Focusing. The next chapter will discuss the basic attitudes that enable Consciousness Focusing to work most rapidly.

*A more detailed description of how to apply the Living Love Methods in your everyday life is contained in *Gathering Power Through Insight and Love* by Ken and Penny Keyes. It is available in bookstores or from the Ken Keyes College Bookroom, 790 Commercial Ave., Coos Bay, Oregon 97420 for $6.95 plus $1.25 for shipping and handling. See Appendix 5 for more information.

A life SAVER....
WHEN YOU ARE DROWNING

STEP I: EXPLORE THE SUFFERING.

1. Take several deep breaths; close your eyes; tune in to your feelings; let yourself really experience them.

2. Mentally re-create a factual objective picture of the scene you were involved in just before you experienced the most intense emotions. Who is involved? Where is it happening? What is happening? What is being said?

3. Now put yourself back in that scene and consciously experience the emotions you are generating:

a. Tune in to your body. Describe the physical sensations. Describe the feelings. Exactly what emotions are you experiencing? Name them: fear, anger, disappointment, etc.

b. Get in touch with your interpretation of the incident. Ask yourself, "What words are going through my mind? What am I telling myself that is producing these emotions?"

c. To get in touch with the basic insecurities that underlie addictive demands, ask yourself: "What is it that is bothering me the most?" "What is the worst thing that could happen?"

STEP II: PINPOINT THE ADDICTION.

1. At the time of the incident, how did you want things to be? What programmed attitudes or models did you have of how you should be, of how others should be, of how the drama "should" have been played?

2. To find the deeper underlying addictive demands, ask yourself: "If things go the way I want and my programmed model is fulfilled, what do I get?" "If I don't get what I want and my model of how things should be is not fulfilled, what does it mean about me?" "How do I feel about myself?"

3. Now pinpoint your principal addictive demand or demands by asking yourself: "In this situation, exactly what am I addictively demanding?" "What do I think I have to have in order to be happy?"

STEP III: SELECT YOUR REPROGRAMMING PHRASES.

1. Do you see how this addiction makes you act like a robot that responds automatically?

IN NEGATIVE, SEPARATING EMOTIONS

2. Do you see how you are making yourself suffer because of this addiction?

3. Can you see the repeated pattern of suffering that this addiction has created in your life?

4. Have you had enough suffering? Are you willing to let go of the demand? If not, make sure that the demand which you chose is what is really bothering you in that situation and repeat Step III.

5. To change the old programming, choose one or two short, pithy reprogramming phrases that counteract specific demands. Thus to counteract the demand for approval, the phrase "I don't need approval" would be appropriate. To counteract a demand not to make mistakes, "I don't have to reject myself if I make mistakes" would help. They should feel right when said rapidly with intensity.

6. Prepare to reprogram by replaying the scene and re-experiencing your emotions. Really get in touch with the suffering your addictions have caused you and with your determination to get free. Let your energy build for a drive toward freedom!

STEP IV: FOCUS ON REPROGRAMMING.

1. Close your eyes. Take ten deep, rapid breaths. Tense your muscles. Build up all the emotional energy you can.

2. Then reprogram with intensity and power. Repeat your reprogramming phrases with gut-level determination until you feel that they have clicked into your biocomputer.

3. To get helpful insights, read the Twelve Pathways aloud and look at the Centers of Consciousness you are using.

4. Put yourself back in the same scene—this time with the new programming in operation. Reaffirm the new programming by visualizing yourself responding to the situation with new positive responses and feelings based on your new programming. Reaffirm that you can be free of old programming—free to be how you really want to be in order to enjoy all of your life.

The conscious, loving energies of Norma Lewis and Kris Nevius have made important contributions in developing the above reprogramming guide.

15
TECHNIQUES OF CONSCIOUSNESS FOCUSING

There are background attitudes and skills that increase the effectiveness of Consciousness Focusing. This chapter will discuss practical things that will help you to use this Method to reprogram addictions. But first let's review the four steps of Consciousness Focusing:

1. **Explore the suffering.**
2. **Pinpoint the addiction.**
3. **Select your reprogramming phrases.**
4. **Focus your consciousness on reprogramming.**

Bearing in mind these steps, here are ways you can improve your effectiveness as you use this Fifth Method:

Welcome the people and situations that can help you become clearly and strongly aware of your addictions.

Usually you carefully protect yourself from people you "just can't stand." You run the other way when life gives you a relationship that worries you. When you begin to work on yourself through the Method of Consciousness Focusing, you try never again to retreat from any person or any life situation as long as it makes you aware of your addictions. You welcome and honor that situation, for it provides you with a continuous input from the outside world that makes you aware of emotional programming you must change in order to uplevel your consciousness. The Method of Consciousness Focusing cannot be used when you are peaceful, serene, and loving. It can only be used effectively at those moments when your existing emotional programming is creating in you feelings of duality and separateness and destroying your capacity to love.

> **Whatever you tell yourself at this time is absolutely crucial. So be sure to blame all of your uptightness on your addictive programming.**

You must change the way you talk to yourself about your life situations so that you no longer imply that anything outside of you is the immediate cause of your unhappiness. Instead of saying, "Joe makes me mad," say, "I make myself mad when I'm around Joe." Instead of saying, "Mary irritates me when she is late," say, "By not showing up on time, Mary continually reminds me that I'm addicted to punctuality." This enables you to use the Method of Consciousness Focusing to gradually get rid of that part of your programming that makes you uptight when something does not conform to your expectations.

It is important to be *very specific and accurate* when you use Consciousness Focusing to reprogram your unconscious levels. *Whatever you tell yourself when you are emotionally upset will play a part in the programming that you will have to live with in the future.* If you make the conventional mistake of blaming the outside world, *you will simply strengthen your addictions.* If you say things that separate you from the outside world such as, "Men are terrible," "Women are awful," you will be programming yourself in a way that will alienate you rather than unite you with the world. If you keep talking to yourself like that, you may develop a cancerous cynicism—and that certainly is not working toward love and oneness. The world is what it is—why make yourself upset about it? Instead of saying, "The cities are horrible," tell yourself, "I must release myself from that part of my emotional programming that makes me upset when I experience certain things in cities." *In other words, you must stop telling yourself that the reason for your up-*

tightness and unhappiness is "out there"—when the truth of the matter is that it is simply your inside programming that continually keeps you uptight. When you have reprogrammed the addiction, then you can choose to put your energy into changing things in the most effective way—and stop putting energy into things which you cannot change.

What you feelingly tell yourself at this crucial time when you are emotionally disturbed is the essence of Consciousness Focusing. *Everything you tell yourself when you are emotionally upset is vital in programming.* You could program yourself to hate everyone by repeatedly telling yourself when you are upset, "Everyone is out to get me." You can program this in your mind so tightly that it will alter your perception of everyone you see. If you want to love people, you can use this opportunity to put in "love programming." Just tell yourself, "I'm tired of being outside of it all. I want to learn to love everyone—no more duality and separateness for me. I've got to learn how to love unconditionally—without demands."

When people are emotionally upset and they continually tell themselves alienating things, *they program themselves directly into neurosis or psychosis.* When you are emotionally upset and use this opportunity to program yourself with the positive ways of Living Love, you wipe out vulnerabilities you programmed in the past.

To summarize: when you are upset, it is vital that you be *extremely precise* in putting the blame for your unhappiness *exactly where it belongs.* Your problems are not in the outside world. They are an interaction between your inside programming and the here and now realities of your body, mind, and the people and situations outside you. Since the outside realities are only minimally changeable by you, your happiness depends on your concentrating on *changing what you can change—your emotional programming* that automatically makes you uptight when the world does not live up to your expectations. Seize every moment of anger, resentment, worry, frustration, anxiety, jealousy, or fear as a precious opportunity to start talking straight to yourself, so that you will no longer get uptight no matter what happens in the world around you.

Find the phrases and thoughts that generate the strongest

emotions when you are upset.

If you wish to use the Method of Consciousness Focusing to get free for your lifetime from an addictive program, it is important to search for all of the phrases and thoughts that intensify your turbulent feelings. Force yourself to experience your emotions in the strongest way. Tell yourself, for example, "I'm sick and tired of getting angry all the time. It's hell to be an automatic robot that stupidly triggers these silly emotional binges. I want to be free of all this idiocy. It's silly for me to be smothered by all this."

Be specific. For example, if jealousy is your problem, tell yourself, "I don't want to be trapped in jealous feelings ever again." Get into the trapped feeling and keep hunting for phrases that trigger strong feelings. When you find a phrase that intensifies your feelings and makes you cry, *keep repeating it over and over until it no longer brings a response.* Find other phrases and *wear them out.* Then go back to test again their ability to trigger strong emotions.

Remember, you must really want to do it. When you reprogram, don't hesitate to yell to yourself, to beat a pillow, to clench your fists and teeth, to pound on a bed or table, or do anything else that gives notice to your ego and your rational mind that you are firmly determined to change your programming. Remember that many of these addictions have been operating in your biocomputer for ten, twenty, thirty or more years, and it is going to take a lot of determination and work on your part to get them reprogrammed so that you are no longer automatically irritated by certain situations.

It is important to use reprogramming phrases which "feel right" to you. Reprogramming phrases should represent new insights you have gained while examining yourself and the situation which you found upsetting. By using the Pathways or the Centers of Consciousness, you may come to realize, for instance, that being criticized is not really a threat to you or harmful in any way. You may begin to perceive criticism as valuable feedback which may help you improve your performance. To reinforce this new attitude toward criticism and make it a permanent part of your programming, it is valuable to reprogram yourself with such phrases as "Criticism is really useful, not harmful" or "I can welcome criticism" or "I don't need to get defensive when someone criticizes me."

If you use reprogramming phrases that don't "feel right" or that you do not consciously believe, you may find yourself experiencing increased resistance as you use the phrase. Instead of feeling relieved, free, and more confident as you reprogram yourself, you may feel increasingly tense and upset. If so, it is best to listen to the arguments your mind is coming up with in opposition to the reprogramming phrase and use the other methods or repeat the procedure on pages 98 and 99 (A LIFE SAVER) to get additional insights. It may be you are not ready to drop a certain demand. You might change the reprogramming phrase slightly into one that feels more appropriate to you. Thus if "I don't have to have a lover" doesn't feel right, you might try "I don't need so-and-so to be happy" or "I don't need to feel hurt when I'm not with so-and-so."

Don't get ahead of yourself into a phony space. Wait until you really feel ready to drop a demand or an unconstructive way of reacting to a situation. When you realize you don't really need something you thought you needed, you will find it easier to drop the addictive demand for it. When you have clearly seen the absurdity of your old programming, effective reprogramming phrases will spontaneously come to you.

Here are some sample reprogramming instructions to your biocomputer that you may find helpful: "Life is my teacher." "I am not my addictive programming." "I am loveable." "I am the master of my life." "I don't need to control people." "I can accept what is." "I don't need other people's approval." "It's okay to make a mistake." "It's okay to be me." "I don't need to hide." "I have nothing to fear." "I can let go and just be." "I love myself." "It's okay to make a fool of myself in public." "Rational mind—stop sending me that stuff." "I am enough." "I accept my here and now." "I don't have to reject myself when I (whichever applies) am angry, make a mistake, feel jealous, am not loving." "It's OK to be right where I am." "I am getting free." "I don't have to be a robot." "I don't have to be uptight when this happens." "I don't have to get caught up in his/her programming." "I can love him/her just the way he/she is." "It's all US." "I don't need (whichever applies) outside acceptance, approval, respect, love, special attention, romantic love, close relationships, to control, to manipulate, to be addicted, to be afraid."

Make up your own phrases to fit your situation. As you become expert in reprogramming, you may be surprised by its effectiveness. With persistence and determination, you can reprogram all of your addictions—no matter how long-standing or how strong they are.

In one Consciousness Focusing session you cannot wipe out all your undesired programming from the past years because you are usually upset about only one thing at a time. You can only reprogram that which is making you upset here and now. So talk specifically to yourself *only about the problem that is making you feel bad right now*. Suppose you relied on someone to help you and he forgot to do what he had agreed to do. You have made yourself angry. Now talk to yourself specifically about that situation: "I don't have to feel angry when I feel people aren't meeting agreements." "I don't need to put myself through all of this turmoil." "People don't have to live up to my models." "I can enjoy what I do have."

Talk very precisely to yourself, *for the feelings you experience when you are upset are the feelings that will be programmed in some degree into your future*. Say things like, "I can reprogram this addiction. I don't need to get uptight over this situation. It's just my programming that is making me uptight. I can change that programming. That programming doesn't serve me in any way. I don't need it for anything. I don't need to hold on to that emotional reaction. Love is more important. I am creating this suffering in my mind. It's all in my mind."

As a way of exploring your suffering (Step 1), you may wish to consciously play out your old programming.

It is helpful to distinguish between *discharging old programming* and *creating new programming*. When you consciously relive a disturbing situation and scream, "I hate you, I hate you!" *with the full intention of getting rid of such garbage from your mind*, you are not reinforcing negative programming; you are freeing yourself from it. Whenever your ego and rational mind *automatically* justify a negative emotion, you tend to perpetuate it. But when you re-live a disturbing situation and consciously discharge the emotions for the purpose of getting rid of them, you help free yourself from the addictive programming. Your biocomputer may receive new, constructive programming more readily when the old programming has been consciously run through and seen as unnecessary. The *conscious* discharge of addictive programming can generate energy that may be useful in getting ready for Consciousness Focusing.

It may be helpful to re-experience what you were telling yourself that caused you to generate these separating emotions. You might have created fear by telling yourself, "It would be terrible if I failed this exam." Sorrow might have been created by telling yourself, "I can't bear to live without Jane. I feel all alone." Anger is generated by thoughts like, "He has no right to treat me that way. Who does he think I am?" You can fully re-live the situation by expressing all these emotion generating statements with full intensity while at the same time clearly realizing that *you are merely discharging old programming* (like dumping out the garbage). The game is to see through it and develop new and better ways of responding to such situations.

Build up the voltage of your emotional responses.

The effective use of the Method of Consciousness Focusing requires you to generate the strongest emotions that you can. Do everything you can to increase the electrochemical voltage of your emotional response. Most of your addictions were programmed into you through suffering and pain. One way to reprogram them is to use the tension that is associated with your stronger feelings. You may be able to get rid of a strong lifetime addiction in a short time—if, and only if, you can build up your emotional intensity. If you cannot get into your emotions strongly and continuously, it may take months or years to reprogram the addiction.

Cry as much as possible—for crying helps you to reprogram faster. Although crying is not essential, it may be the easiest way to build up the intensity needed for reprogramming rapidly. As you cry, keep telling yourself, "I don't have to hassle myself with this. I don't need separating emotions. I can be free of this demand. I don't have to hold on." The longer you cry and focus your consciousness on eliminating the addiction, the more you will be able to effectively eliminate the programming that makes you upset with that particular situation in your life.

It is not necessary to cry in order to reprogram, but it speeds up the process. Since much of your emotional programming was put into you through shock, pain, crying, and suffering, remember that it helps *to consciously build up your present pain, crying, and suffering* so that you can rapidly wipe out this programming.

Don't let any person or any of your thoughts cool you down. Stop only when you just can't keep the emotion churning any longer. It could be helpful to have someone with you who quietly hears you, *but says nothing.* Most people when they are with someone who is crying will say, "Everything will be all right. Let's dry your tears," or they suggest some type of diversion. But this stops you from using the Consciousness Focusing Method to burn out the unconscious-level programming that is making you suffer. If you start *doing* things, *you will be using your senses and rational mind to smother the problem.* It will temporarily make you feel good but it will leave you in the grip of your automatic programming when similar situations come up in the future. Anyone who is with you should understand what you are doing. She or he should simply experience your vibrations and *silently* encourage you to cry. Do everything possible to build up your emotional intensity. For when you build up the emotional intensity, you have a great opportunity to reprogram an addiction so that you no longer get yourself emotionally upset when certain things happen in the outside world.

Develop the confidence that you can absolutely be the master of yourself.

Keep telling yourself that you programmed yourself many years ago and that you can reprogram that which you programmed. Remember that *you did it all to yourself.* You are not in the grip of forces beyond your control! It's all in your mind. Through the Method of Consciousness Focusing, you can be the master of your mind. You are a perfect being—pure Conscious-awareness. Your only problem is that you are caught in the grip of too many things that you are telling yourself you must have to be happy. You are laying too many conditions on the outside world that it (and the people in it) cannot possibly meet. You are culture-bound. You have programmed yourself with all these addictions, demands, and expectations—and you can reprogram yourself. When you have reprogrammed your addictions, you are free for a lifetime. All the happiness and the beauty of the world will then be yours.

It doesn't matter if you feel that everything you have tried in life has failed. It doesn't matter what particular hell you are in at this moment. If you are together enough to be reading a book on the Living Love Way to Higher Consciousness, you can use the Method of Consciousness Focusing. You have everything you need to work on yourself and you can positively reprogram yourself to eliminate all the hellish emotions that keep you from enjoying your life continuously.

Your emotion-backed addictions will not disappear the first time you use the Consciousness Focusing Method, but with each successive application of the Method you will gradually change an addiction to a preference. A complex addiction (such as an addiction to sex) has many different addictive triggers that will require separate sessions of Consciousness Focusing. Be patient and give yourself time to get results. It is not helpful to say or think at a disturbed moment, "This reprogramming is not working." You could program your reprogramming not to work! Instead, say or think, "Slowly, but surely, I am getting free of these emotional triggers." *You* put these neural connections in your head and with determination *you can get them out.*

The Living Love Way to Higher Consciousness thus offers you Five Methods that are designed to enable all types of people to reprogram all kinds and intensities of addictions. If you wish to accelerate your journey into higher consciousness, work hard to develop the maximum skill at using all of the Five Methods. You will then find that your biocomputer will automatically select the Method that is just perfect for each reprogramming problem.

At first you may be fascinated by understanding the workings of your consciousness from the vantage point of the Twelve Pathways, the Seven Centers, and the Five Methods. You may then get into consciously using these tools in a minute-to-minute fashion. The purpose of these tools is to enable you to tune in to the nowness of life—free from the distortions caused by addictions. As they begin to work for you, your life will begin to smooth out.

Learn to enjoy your life! Just use the Methods when you are aware of some expectations in your life that are not in harmony with what is here and now. In other words, you use them for troubleshooting—and the rest of the time you are just right here enjoying doing your thing. *The main purpose of these tools is to help you to stop doing these things that divide you from other people and the world around you—to accept and love one another and flow in that space where there is just "us"—right here—right now.*

16
THE INSTANT CONSCIOUSNESS DOUBLER

The Instant Consciousness Doubler can help you sidestep many of your addictions. Most of the time a major expansion of your consciousness requires a lot of continuous inner work, but there is one shortcut through the woods that may be called an Instant Consciousness Doubler. Since consciousness and love are synonymous, you might also consider this an Instant Love Doubler.

Here are the directions for making a significant instant expansion of your consciousness:

> **Expand your love, your consciousness, and your loving compassion by experiencing everything that everyone does or says as though you had done or said it.**

When you use this Instant Consciousness Doubler, you will bring into play a certain programming in your biocomputer that you may not consciously use now in responding to the actions and words of other people. You are usually aware of some of the *inside reasons and feelings* that account for what *you* do. But when you perceive similar behavior in another person, you usually interpret it with different programming than you use for experiencing *your own thoughts and actions.*

This leads us into such psychological conjugations as, "I am firm, you are obstinate, he is pigheaded." "I am frank, you are blunt, he is rude." "I enjoy my food, you overeat, he is a glutton." "I occasionally correct people for their own good, you are quite argumentative, he has a terrible temper." In all of the above situations *the external actions could have been the same,* but the programming that you use to interpret the situation is entirely different.

The purpose of the Instant Consciousness Doubler is to remind you to use the same programming in perceiving and interpreting the actions and words of other people *that you use in understanding your own actions and words.* If you simply delay your response to each situation long enough to run it through the programming you reserve for yourself, you may find that your ability to understand and love other people will instantly double. You may be able to simply bypass the old programming and let it gradually wither away from disuse. You begin to realize that you would probably feel and say the same things that other people are doing and saying if you could just stand in their shoes and see things from their point of view.

To use the Instant Consciousness Doubler, you *consciously* feed the situation in through the programming that you use when crystallizing your perception of your own feelings and actions. In many situations this can instantly double your perceptiveness and wisdom in responding acceptingly and lovingly to everyone around you. Almost every time you feel irritated or angry, you are simply alienating yourself from another person who is probably doing *exactly the same thing that you've done thousands of times—and which you may have accepted fully in yourself.*

Suppose, for example, you ask someone to do something for you and he replies in an irritated way, "Why don't you do it yourself?" When these words come in through your auditory nerves and are fed into the interpretive sections of your biocomputer, you are very likely to experience a threat to your Power Center. This is the point at which you use the Instant Consciousness Doubler. You can say to yourself, "There have been many times when I've been annoyed when someone asked me to do something. Perhaps I was busy. Perhaps I felt that they could do it easier and better than I, and they should not be asking me in the first place. Or perhaps I was tired. Perhaps my addictions were at that moment keeping me from loving them enough to want to be helpful. I can furnish myself with dozens of reasons for not wanting to help people when I'm asked to."

How soon
will you realize
that the only thing
you don't have is
the direct experience

that there's
nothing you need

that you
don't have?

When you use the Instant Consciousness Doubler, you give other people the benefit of all the inside understanding that you use to forgive yourself when you respond in an alienating way. And so instead of becoming angry when someone refuses to help, you use the Instant Consciousness Doubler to perceive it in a broader perspective that lets you accept it and love the person. This helps to free you from the dualistic programming that is used for perceiving the actions of "other" people.

The Instant Consciousness Doubler helps us realize that there are no "others" in this world. All of us have shared the same feelings, the same problems of being dominated by our security, sensation and power addictions, and the same needs for love and oneness. When we experience this with here-and-now awareness, could we feel anything but love and acceptance for all of our brothers and sisters?

17
YOUR RATIONAL MIND

For most people, life is a battleground between the outside world and their security, sensation, and power-dominated egos. To experience the beauty of life, it is necessary for one's mind to return to the gentle calmness that most infants enjoy much of the time. To continually appreciate your life from the Fourth, Fifth, or Sixth Centers of Consciousness, you do not have to train yourself to the point where thoughts do not spontaneously occur and there is no random stream of consciousness. However, the urgency, stridency, and insistency of your stream of thoughts must be slowed down to the pace of a very light breeze that gently moves the leaves of a tree—instead of a forceful, gusty wind that whips and bends the branches back and forth.

When you were born, you had very few emotion-backed demands. Some milk when hungry was the main one. Since that time, you have programmed yourself with hundreds and hundreds of emotion-backed demands that have nothing to do with physiologically maintaining your life. Most of these addictions are concerned with the social dance of living out the various roles we emotionally attach ourselves to. An emotion-backed addictive model or expectation is like an inflated balloon that you always keep with you and that you have to constantly guard to keep someone from popping it. While your ego is busy mistakenly trying to protect you by automatically triggering your security fears, sensation longings, and power angers, your rational mind churns away trying to do its part in support of the ego. It furnishes reasons why you are "right" and the other person is "wrong." It manipulates and schemes to help you live out your model of "success" in the various roles and dramas with which you are identifying yourself.

As you grow toward higher consciousness, you begin to realize that all of the fear, grief, and anger that you experience is simply a teaching that the world is offering you to help you free yourself from this hollow dance you are doing. The world is giving you the experience that will help you develop an insight into the mechanical way you are acting out various addictive roles. Every feeling of alienation, resentment, distrust, or irritation *with anything anyone does or says* should be viewed as a reminder that you are not consciously playing the game of your life. The world is telling you that

Life is just a game we play—
and there is no special way!

Your ego and your rational mind labor under the harsh programming that there is a certain special way the world should be and the people around you should act—and it is up to your rational mind to put it all aright. When your life presents you with something that does not fit your addictive models, your ego sparks the rational mind into an insistent, grabbing chain of thoughts. Simultaneously the ego triggers negative emotions such as anxiety or resentment. Your heart begins to beat faster, and adrenalin and other hormones are introduced into your bloodstream. This psychosomatic turmoil feeds back into your rational mind and sparks even further activity. Unless you understand how your consciousness works, you accept this turmoil as something "important" that must be attended to in order to make your life work. As you become more conscious, you develop the ability to let your rational mind do its thing without automatically taking you into a burst of emotional turmoil that makes you try to manipulate and coerce the outside world to fit your expectations.

For example, when you have no perspective on the activities of that trio consisting of your addictive programming, your ego, and your rational mind, you automatically get angry if someone criticizes you. When your Power Center of Consciousness no longer operates to generate your response, you begin to have a choice of what to do and say when someone criticizes you. You may wish to just quietly hear what they say and express appreciation for their caring enough to give you the benefit of their thoughts. It is not always necessary for you to agree or disagree—just receive what is offered and use what you can use and let the rest pass by. You may wish to discuss or clarify people's criticisms and suggestions. You may wish to ask them to help you in some way—and they may be willing to put energy into what they are suggesting. You may wish to tell them that you have already considered accomplishing what they are mentioning, and you just simply made the decision to do it the way you have done it and "that is where it is at" right here and now. In other words, when you are receptive and conscious, rather than hyper-reactive and irritated, you have a choice of responses.

This instant, automatic alarm system (in which your programming, ego, and rational mind create an emotional feeling of urgency) was designed to bring our ancestors through the perils of jungle life. Unless you are confronted with a situation involving immediate physical injury or a threat to your life, the optimal solution to any "problem" is usually found best by harmonizing your energies with the energies of the world around you. And to flow harmoniously in an "us" consciousness (instead of a "me vs. them" consciousness), it is necessary to be quiet enough to get in touch with the insight and perceptiveness that will always come to you when you uplevel your addictions to preferences.

As you become more and more proficient in using the Pathways, you begin to see clearly the game that your rational mind has been playing on you. You will see the way that it gets pulled into the act by both your addictive programming and your ego to produce long chains of critical, alienating thoughts. And you learn to label these thoughts that you generate when you are upset as pure nonsense. You don't accept them—and you don't reject them. You just let them happen, watch them, and experience how peaceful it is not to be emotionally caught up in them any longer. This enables the intuitive wisdom that is always within you to emerge.

Suppose, for example, that someone urges you to change your mind about something. You may experience that your power, prestige, and pride boundaries are being violated. Your rational mind will be activated by your ego to produce a forceful retort to completely devastate the person who is so stupid as to disagree with you. When you are able to watch your mind do its thing, without triggering negative emotional feelings, you will then have a choice as to which response produces division, and which produces love and oneness. When you are operating on lower consciousness levels, you have no choice. You tend to immediately utter every "urgent thought" that comes into your mind—even if it means interrupting another person. As you grow into higher consciousness, you are able to simply observe the computer-like, automated "printout" that is taking place in your rational mind. You view it as a sixth sense—as just another sensory input. By upleveling your addictions into preferences, your thoughts no longer cause your emotions to automatically flare up. You begin for the first time in your life to be liberated from the dance of your rational mind.

It is interesting to note that this is not repression. When you repress, you do not express what you are feeling because you are afraid of the consequences. Repression is one of the most unconscious and harmful things you can do to yourself. What we are suggesting is that you take the energy generated by an emotion and turn this into reprogramming the addiction into a preference. You thus do not repress the energy, but you actually use it constructively and beneficially so that your rational chains of thought do not trigger feelings of anger or resentment. As you become more conscious, *there will be no negative emotions to repress—or even to express.* You become literally like a connoisseur who does not just grab any food, but who, in a discriminating way, uses insight and perceptiveness to consciously choose. A conscious being knows that life always works best when we operate from a loving space that lets us receive and experience other people (no matter what they do or say) as no different from ourselves.

When your biocomputer begins processing all incoming visual, auditory, and other data in ways that do not keep you irritated and upset, you find that the screen of your consciousness is no longer dominated by a constant conflict between you and the outside world. You are then able to tune in to the more subtle aspects of the people and situations around you. Your insight and perceptiveness increase a hundredfold. You find that your inherent wisdom (which can be drawn upon only to the degree that your rational mind is calm) guides you so that you are able to produce the optimal response to every situation in your life.

A traditional way of calming the rational mind is through meditation. Most types of meditation involve sitting with spine erect in a quiet room and continuously focusing your attention on a physical object or a mental concept in order to crowd out random thoughts. For example, you may concentrate on experiencing your breathing in and breathing out. Or you could just put a lighted candle in front of you and train your consciousness to be dominated completely and continuously during the meditation period by only the candle flame. When random thoughts come, such as, "I wonder how long this is going to take to really get results," or, "My right knee doesn't feel right," you do not stay with the thoughts and permit them to free-associate. You do not, however, reject these thoughts—for the harder you reject them, the more they will hold on tenaciously. You gradually develop the ability to just let them go by, and you gently and constantly return to the object of your meditation. You know that only one thing can dominate the central stage of your consciousness at any one time with full attention—although your mind can switch back and forth to different matters in a fraction of a second. By continually keeping one object or thought in your consciousness, you can gradually train your mind to calm down its random dance so that it can be a more enjoyable and pleasant servant for you.

If you are now using a traditional method of meditation and are getting results from it, it may be preferable for you to continue this practice—especially if you have a good meditation teacher with whom you work personally. Any system of meditation is in harmony with the Living Love Way. However, if you do not use a particular method of meditation at this time, you may wish to use the Five Methods described in this book to calm your mind during your period of growth into the Fourth Center. These Five Methods of the Living Love Way do not require you to turn off the world even for an hour, or to detach yourself from your everyday activities. They enable you to develop a capacity *for achieving many of the benefits of meditation while you are busily engaged in the activities of your life.* One of the main objects of meditation is to experience yourself and the world around you clearly and consciously —free from emotion-backed demands, attachments, addictive models, childhood conditioning, etc. For many people we feel that the most *direct* way to do this is through working with the Twelve Pathways, the Seven Centers, and the Five Methods. We like to consider these techniques as a form of "meditation in action."

Calming your rational mind by reducing the load of addictions that keep it activated is an important phase of your growth into higher consciousness. Since we have an animal background of millions of years in the jungle where life or death depended upon split-second timing, *our emotions, egos, and rational minds are far too reactive to what is going on around us.* As you grow toward higher consciousness, you become more receptive and accepting. You just let the sensory stuff come in—and you let it sort itself out and drift on by. You see the "warnings" being generated by your rational mind, but you have learned to let your mind produce its stream of thoughts without getting your ego caught up in them. When your mind generates security, sensation, and power-motivated thoughts that make you feel alienated and you begin to throw someone out of your heart, you know that you are operating on the lower levels of consciousness. You become increasingly aware of times when your rational mind is churning and speeding. You are determined not to lose your tuned-in insight into the here and now and your ability to love unconditionally. Then any action you engage in will be effective and produce the optimal results both now and in the future.

The love and peace of higher consciousness flow from just

being—and enjoying it all. Anything you *do* will not be enough unless you feel fulfilled in *just being*. Usually we are not happy when we finish *doing* whatever it is that we think we have to do. Doing creates expectations that your world and the people around you may or may not fit. The things we *do* disappear in time. We must learn to appreciate just being alive in the nowness of whatever situation we are in.

Contentment is not only a benefit of higher consciousness but it is also one of the ways of working toward higher consciousness. Just insist that your rational mind slow down its rejection of the here and now, with its endless churnings, comparisons, and judgments that usually create the experience of otherness. There are times when you may have to forcefully tell your rational mind to "shut up" so that you can enjoy your here and now. As we pointed out in the story of the Zen monk, tigers, and strawberries, there are always things you can think about to keep your rational mind and emotions stirred up. And there are always the "strawberries" to be enjoyed right here and now. Whether you enjoy your life continuously, or constantly harass yourself, depends upon how well you learn to simply change what is changeable without throwing people out of your heart—and then quietly accept that which you cannot change except by heavy subject-object manipulation and force.

In becoming aware of how your rational mind operates to alienate you from people, you will need to watch for the "chain-reaction effect." Let's suppose you enjoy being with a person and you have many things in common that draw you together. Then suppose you have one strong addiction that leads you to be angry and throw this person out of your heart. Unless you can quickly get on top of this addiction and become more conscious, you will find that the alienating attitude triggered by your addiction *will spread like a cancer and cause you to become critical of this person in other ways that have nothing to do with the original addiction.* Your rational mind is simply prostituting itself to the unconscious workings of the ego and your addictive programming. You will begin to feel separate and alien toward this person in one way after another.

Your rational mind will check back in the memory files and begin to reinterpret past events to "cast a new light on them"—purporting to show that the relationship really wasn't as beautiful as it seemed at the time. It will carefully rehash both the past and the present in the light of your other security, sensation, and power addictions and will tend to blow up little things into big separating "problems."

For example, let's suppose Tom and Mary are married, and they have a mutually loving, flowing relationship. Suppose Tom needs to go to a night-and-day business conference in a city a thousand miles away. Since he will be busy all the time, he prefers not to take Mary with him. Suppose Mary has an addiction for going on this trip with Tom. Her Power Center of Consciousness is demanding that Tom not leave her at home alone overnight. Unless she can become conscious of what she is doing to herself with this emotion-backed addictive model, her rational mind may suggest to her that Tom is getting tired of her, Tom wants to have an affair with someone else, Tom is on a heavy power trip and does not really love her, the rest of their lives together will probably be clouded by Tom's leaving her at home more and more often, perhaps Tom is ashamed of her and doesn't want his business associates to meet her, etc., etc. There is no end to the nonsense that the rational mind can spin out as the pawn of the ego. A person growing into higher consciousness learns to spot this sewer-like churning and spewing and refuses to let the rational mind's activity trigger any negative emotions. You may expect to have many real battles with your rational mind in order to stay conscious.

Just like any complex machine, our rational mind can make a beautiful contribution to our well-being if we are keenly sensitive to its limitations and problem areas. The techniques of the Living Love Way will enable you to become an expert "trouble-shooter" so that your rational mind can work for you—and not against you. Your rational mind is a master at proving that you are "right"—and the other person is "wrong." But in order to be a conscious, loving, happy, and fulfilled being, *it is not enough to be "right."* You can be "right" in your individual contracts and in your performance of society's games—and live a thoroughly miserable, alienated, unhappy life. We all know people who are "correct" and "right" almost all of the time—and the lives of these people do not work to produce happiness. *It's much more fulfilling to be loved than to be "right."* **Love brings more happiness than efficiency.** It's often better to give other people space to find their own errors or to let the natural chain of events in their life show them where they have to change. If a person asks you if you think he is right, you should then open yourself completely and give him the benefit of your thoughts and feelings. But arguing at every opportunity in order to convince people that you are right and others are wrong simply means that you are trapped by your rational mind and are unconsciously and mechanically acting out your security, sensation, and power addictions.

A Zen master had a beautiful young lady as his pupil. She became pregnant, and she falsely named her teacher as the father of her child. When the child was born, her family indignantly brought the child to the Zen master and accused him of taking advantage of his beautiful young pupil. His only reply was, "Ah—so." They left the child with the Zen master, who enjoyed caring for it and had many beautiful hours playing with the child. After about a year the young lady was very ill, and not wanting to die with this false accusation on her conscience, she told her family that the real father was a young man who lived in a nearby town. Her mother and father immediately went to the teacher and profoundly bowed and apologized and asked for the baby back. The Zen master gave them the baby and said, "Ah—so."

When they first accused him, the rational mind of the Zen master did not get caught up in a big chain of ego-backed arguments indignantly denying that he was the father, protesting that he was unjustly accused, threatening to tell people about the lie that was being perpetrated upon him, etc. He realized that a mother and father are not likely to believe the word of a man against the word of their pregnant daughter. He simply saw that they were not open and did not want to hear his side of it. *They did not ask him whether he had done it*—they accusingly told him he had done it. And so the Zen master simply flowed with the drama being enacted and did not agree or disagree. He stayed in a peaceful state of higher consciousness and simply enjoyed what was going on—and he was able to have the fun of living with the baby for a while. When they came back and apologized for their false accusations, his rational mind did not say, "I could have told you, but you wouldn't have listened." He simply peacefully saw that they now understood and there was nothing to be said. He could continue to enjoy the new act in the drama.

This story does not tell us that we must never give our side of things in any situation. It simply says that when you are conscious, *you have a choice as to whether to get in a discussion because you know in advance whether the argument will bring you and the other person into a closer state of love and oneness or whether it will separate you.* Under the circumstances, the Zen master's reply, "Ah—so," was the best reply to produce the closest harmony that could be obtained in that situation. Later he willingly and lovingly gave the child up without recriminations. For all concerned this also represented a flowingly harmonious thing to do. Most people with whom you interact will be more open than the parents of the pregnant girl. Usually you will be able to use the Seventh Pathway, which tells you to open yourself completely to other people. But also use the Ninth Pathway, to open yourself in a centered, calm, and loving way.

As you learn to increasingly identify yourself with your Conscious-awareness, you will find that your rational mind becomes a useful tool that is somewhat on a par with your other senses. In conjunction with your stored memories, it is the sense that produces hypotheses, theories, conjectures, and possibilities. You know that just as your eyes or ears can mislead you, your rational mind can equally mislead you.*

*For further help in developing your thinking ability see *Taming Your Mind* by Ken Keyes, Jr. This book is available in bookstores or from Ken Keyes College Bookroom, 790 Commercial Ave., Coos Bay, Oregon 97420. The cost is $7.95 plus $1.25 for postage and handling. Clothbound edition.

As your addictions are upleveled to preferences, you will find that your senses and your rational mind will have less distortion and will cooperate more to help your life work. You will then be enjoying your birthright as a human being. You will be the master of your emotions, your ego, and your rational mind. This is one of the greatest things any human being can do. It may be beautiful to paint great pictures, erect tall buildings, or write great novels. But to become the master of yourself is an even higher contribution to all mankind—and to yourself as well. And from this place, your external achievement will be even more tuned in to the energy flow of the world.

18

THE ILLUSION OF SELF

There are many paths leading to the top of the mountain of consciousness. It is important for you to find your path—and then stay with that path even when you find the going rough. One of ego's tricks is to make you doubt whether your path will work. It will work—if you will work.

It may be helpful to take a look at three factors that represent aspects of consciousness growth. These factors are systematically intertwined so that *an advance with any one of them will automatically provide a forward step with the other two factors:*

1. **Eliminating your addictive demands.**
2. **Quieting your rational mind.**
3. **Disidentifying with the "self" which your ego guards so constantly.**

The Living Love Way concentrates its techniques on the first factor above. The Five Methods enable you to eliminate addictions that create an "adrenalinized" consciousness which makes you throw people out of your heart. Your addictive demands soak up your energy by making you compulsively run toward things or away from things, destroy your insight and perceptiveness, remove your consciousness from the here and now by keeping you preoccupied with the past and future, and turn off the energy of people around you who might otherwise be able to love and help you.

The Methods of Living Love concentrate on showing you how to make rapid progress in eliminating emotion-backed demands that keep you constantly on the pleasure-pain roller-coaster. When you see the cause-effect relationship between your addictions and your suffering, you can constructively use your suffering to reprogram rapidly. You thus tend to work with a higher level of dynamic energy that you can channel into boosting your rate of consciousness growth. For many people, this is much faster than working directly on quieting the mind or dropping away the self. And since an increase of any one factor accelerates the realization of the other two factors, eliminating your addictions may also be your most rapid technique for calming your mind or knowing what you really are.

One of the great approaches to the mountain of consciousness involves the letting go of the "self" with which we are identifying and which we protect so laboriously. And progress in disidentifying with the myriad of things we contain within our self boundary also helps us quiet the mind and drop away addictive demands.

As children, we learn to experience a territory that we call "myself" or "mine." This "self" is considered to be bounded by our skin, although we experience extentions of the "self" with concepts such as my toys, my room, my dog, my clothes, my friend, my reputation, etc. We feel that everything is *mine* or *not mine*. And we generate the experience of alienation and anger towards people when they appear to encroach on territory we consider our own.

Since the ego is constantly busy protecting the territory it has defined as "mine," it can never relax into the here and now. It must always be securing its future happiness. This continuous activity reinforces the sensation of an "I" or "me" or "self" to whom the territory belongs, and to whom painful experiences are always threatening to happen. One's programming *reinforced by memory* thus forces the ego to continually protect its territory—which it identifies as "self."

The frequency with which one's biocomputer is running off addictive programs creates the illusion that this "I" or "self" is an entity—a "somebody"—rather than a robot-like activity. When this activity of "I" or "self" is recognized as *an activity* rather than an entity, we begin to see that we are responsible for our suffering.

The "I" is this activity of defense. When we stop defending, there is no more "I" or "self."

We work hard to make ourselves suffer. It's a full-time job with no time off even on vacations! As this activity and basic attitude of addictively securing one's future happiness begins to be reprogrammed, the "I" loses its purpose and begins to merge with what is here and now.

Depending on one's security, sensation, and power profile, the self boundary is drawn at different places with different people. For example, a man may defend as a part of himself various patriarchal feelings towards women that involve domination, control, and masculine superiority. Another man may not identify his self boundary with these subject-object relationships, but instead he experiences as essentially like himself all beings who happen to be encased in female bodies. Thus the area that we regard as part of our "self" will fluctuate, depending upon the attitudes and concepts one has acquired and the stage of consciousness development one is in.

If we would understand the nature of this experience that we regard as "myself," it may be helpful to realize that the self boundaries we defend are *like boils on our skin.* A boil is a part of us—*and yet it is not a part of us.* It is just a functional thing that arises and that can pass away. It is not a structural part of our body like our liver or bones or eyes. Like a boil, the self concepts that we pick up in our cultural milieu cause a lot of pain and messiness. And also like a boil on our skin, the "self" will dissolve in its own way as we get healthier.

One might ask, "How could this experience of 'self' be such an impermanent part of us when it is felt so strongly?" Our experience of "self" is created by the frequency with which our ego is defending our security, sensation, and power addictions. Since these lower three Centers of Consciousness determine most of our experience before we begin to grow toward higher consciousness, our minds are moment-by-moment reinforcing the boundaries of this impermanent experience of "self." The waves of the here and now are constantly trying to wash away this boundary of "self" that we are maintaining by our addictions and our stored memories. But we keep drawing a self boundary in the addictive sand of our personality so that it is continually defined and redefined in our experience.

With each addiction that you are successful in upleveling to a preference, you will find that a hunk of this "self" disappears. Instead of experiencing people as objects, you increasingly feel them as "us" or "like me." Gradually, with the upleveling of almost all of your addictions into preferences, this sharply defined experience of "self" leaves you. You then begin to identify with other people even when they do something that previously would have triggered an angry response in you. You just see that they are doing something that you have done hundreds or thousands of times—and you do not throw them out of your heart.

When you are heavily addicted, your experience of "self" is solid like a block of ice. When you have succeeded in reprogramming almost all of your addictions into preferences, your "self" loses its rockness and begins to have the adaptability and clarity of water. When one is operating primarily on preferences, the hardness melts and instead there is a conscious fluidity. In this state, like water, your sense of "self" is infinitely flexible to accommodate itself to your here-and-now surroundings. But there is still a gentle experience of "self" even at the Fourth through Sixth Centers of Consciousness. All of the intense separateness and alienation of the previous rock-like "self" is gone—but a shadow of the former "self" still remains. Since it is now so flexible, and since you have trained your ego not to fire your energy into guarding and defending it, this gentler experience of "self" does not keep you from enjoying a happy life. The self boundary created by your preferential programming enables you to love everyone unconditionally—including yourself.

For the few intrepid explorers of the mountain of consciousness who wish to go to the top (which in the Living Love Way we call the Seventh Center of Consciousness), even preferences must be reprogrammed. The same tools of mindfulness that enable one to get rid of addictions can be used to eliminate preferences. But one should realize that just as the ability to skillfully play the Brahms violin concerto is extremely rare and attainable only by a few people, the ability to reside in the Seventh Center of Consciousness is unusual today. Enjoying life in the Fourth through Sixth Centers of Consciousness is something that almost every one of us can do when we are sufficiently fed up with yo-yoing between pleasure and pain and are determined to use the Five Methods to get free of the addictions which keep us from continuously enjoying life.

At the Seventh Center of Consciousness even the fluid self boundaries disappear. As water evaporates, it becomes a transparent vapor. Similarly, at the highest level of consciousness, the experience of "self" becomes a transparent vapor that does not affect perception or dam up the intuitive wisdom that is within each of us. As our perception of "self" or "somebody" disappears, we become "nobody"—*which then lets us be in a unitive space with everybody.*

And so, step by step, we climb the mountain of consciousness. We find the path that most beckons to us and then we let the cosmic energy within each of us impel us toward the loftier regions where serenity, unconditional love, and fulfillment await us.

19
HOW TO RECOGNIZE YOUR ADDICTIONS

Since the Living Love Way to Higher Consciousness is based on gradually eliminating your addictions, it is most important that you learn to automatically spot them in your moment-to-moment flow of consciousness. A year contains 31,536,000 seconds—each of which offers you an opportunity to grow in consciousness. How fully you benefit from these thirty-one million opportunities is up to you.

You can recognize an addiction by your awareness that your biocomputer is using emotional programming to make you irritated, angry, jealous, confused, tired, bored, defeated, fearful, resentful, or upset in one way or another. Once you are well on your way to reprogramming your more gross addictions, you may then become aware of your subtle addictions. A subtle addiction does not get you upset emotionally—but with a subtle addiction your consciousness is preoccupied with the addiction for a period of minutes, hours, or days.

We may kid ourselves that we are thinking profoundly and continually about a subject, but we're actually churning away most inefficiently and ineffectively—and diverting energy and consciousness that could be more optimally used. As you grow into higher consciousness, your here-and-now broad-channel perception and your relative freedom from having your consciousness dominated by addictions will intuitively give you the wise and effective answer to any problem. As you work toward the higher levels of consciousness, you will find that "thinking" (juggling words, hypotheses, and ideas centering around a problem) is usually not the way to find the optimal solution to your problems. A free, undominated awareness that is highly attuned here and now to the people and situations around you will best enable you to benefit by the wisdom that is waiting to be tapped in your biocomputer. Your problem is to get at the wisdom that you already have—but which is now inaccessible due to your security, sensation, and power-dominated consciousness.

One of the obstacles we must overcome to grow into higher consciousness is the "Spiritual Lawyer" phase. When we first begin our journey and really see the job of reprogramming that awaits us, our ego will experience a threat because of a necessity to change certain lifetime habits that keep us on lower consciousness levels. But then once the ego gets familiar with the rules of the game, it learns how to distort these rules so that we can rationalize our avoiding the Twelve Pathways and other tools for consciousness growth.

Let us suppose that you annoy yourself when someone asks you to repeat something you just told him. Your ego puts your consciousness on the power level by introducing the thought that if the *other* person had given *you* enough of his attention and realized the importance of *your* words, he would have been able to hear *you* clearly the first time. Your ego then tells you that it is important that the other person learn to respect *you* enough to pay attention when *you* speak. You are showing your irritation in order to help him develop better habits of attention. Your ego at that time does not permit you to remember that your uptightness is a sure sign of an addiction (in this case a power addiction) and that you are creating duality and alienation between yourself and the other person. All of us from time to time ask people to repeat what they have said. And so the other person is just doing something that all of us have often done. If we were responding from the Love Center of Consciousness, we would feel no irritation—and simply repeat the information asked for.

To be
upset
over
what
you don't have...

is
to waste
what
you do have

Your ego may find that it can continue to operate as usual and protect the Power Center of Consciousness by twisting some of the Pathways. During the very moments when your curt tones are creating alienation and separation *because you are treating another person as different from yourself,* your ego can be telling you that you're really doing the other person a favor by giving him a chance to use the Third Pathway: "I welcome the opportunity (even if painful) that my minute-to-minute experience offers me to become aware of the addictions I must reprogram to be liberated from my robot-like emotional patterns."

Your ego might even summon up the Twelfth Pathway to justify the duality that you are producing by telling you that you are an awakening being who is here to teach your friend to listen more consciously to your words of wisdom. But, of course, this should be seen as a distortion of the Twelfth Pathway. This Pathway does not place on you the burden of playing God for the benefit of other people! Rather, it tells you, "I am perceiving everyone, including myself, as an awakening being who is here to claim his or her birthright to the higher consciousness planes of unconditional love and oneness." You love and serve an awakening being by doing what he or she asks you to do. If someone asks you to repeat something, you repeat it. In other words, you treat him as a being who is here to help *you* become aware of *your addictions* and get free of them. You avoid letting your ego pump you up into a pseudo-guru who is authorized to dominate or teach others.

When your consciousness is dominated by the lower three levels, *it is the natural flow of your personality that will best teach other people.* It is most important that you realize that any attempt to play God and consciously teach others by deliberately and intentionally giving them dualistic experiences may retard your consciousness growth. It will create alienation between you and other people.

As you grow into higher consciousness levels, you will intuitively feel when a person is open to instruction in consciousness growth. You will either wait until you are clearly aware of this openness or until you are asked to act as teacher. And even then you tell people *only the things they are ready to hear* and can understand with oneness. If they begin to get restless or show continual irritation, you will know that you are not operating from a higher consciousness level that gives only what the other person is prepared to hear. When the requirement of "readiness to hear" is met, that which is given is received so naturally that the person almost feels as if he thought of it himself. In fact, his readiness creates the experience of learning as much as the information of the "giver."

Always remember that the Twelve Pathways will gradually and continually lead you into completely peaceful and loving spaces *no matter what people do or say around you!* If you prefer that something be different from the way it is, you work from the certain knowledge that *love and expanded consciousness* are absolutely enough to lead you to the optimal enjoyment of your life. Your striving, pushing, and dominating can only make surface changes in the way people feel and act. You need to deeply recognize that these superficial changes are usually obtained at a heavy price in alienation and unhappiness. Your forcing usually brings only temporary changes on the surface of behavior. Since real love requires the unconditional acceptance of another person, you are showing that you do not love him because there are conditions he must fulfill before you can love him.

When you can love a person only if he or she is able to act in a fashion that fits your addictive programming, you are treating the other person as an object to be manipulated. When you were growing up, you probably experienced a lot of dominating behavior from your well-meaning parents. You now have ego-backed programming that addictively resists dominating "intrusions" into your life. Of course, as you grow into higher consciousness, you reprogram even these power-resisting addictions, so that dominating behavior on the part of another person is understandingly seen for what it is—his entrapment in the Third Center of Consciousness. Thus you select the communications you find useful, and let the rest quietly go by—and most importantly, you no longer mirror another person's addictive "stuff."

It is important that you deeply perceive that love and expanded consciousness are completely enough to give you everything you need in your life. For example, if you like your coffee cooled before it is given to you to drink, you can use a dominating impatience to "help" your friend remember to put a little water into your coffee so that you can drink it as soon as you get it. If he or she forgets, you may show irritation to help him or her remember—but in so doing you will disturb your peace and serenity. You will also disturb his or her peace and serenity. And you will produce a duality and alienation that slightly dilutes the feelings of love that make the relationship delightful. You need to tell yourself that if you love that person and gently and lovingly communicate what you prefer, she or he will sooner or later remember to make your coffee exactly the way you want it. It is far better for you here and now to lovingly get up and put a little water in your coffee than to engage in alienating emotional behavior. Keep telling yourself that your usual habits of control and domination have never been enough to enable you to find the love, peace, and serenity that you would like in your human relationships. Remind yourself at every opportunity that love and expanded consciousness can be enough—but they must be deep and genuine and flow from your inner being.

There is nothing about higher consciousness that says you *have to become involved in other people's predicaments.* You just learn to love them unconditionally—regardless of what they say or do. You're still entitled to your own choices, and you can steer your boat down the river of your life in any way that you want. Just don't keep crashing into the boats of other people.

Suppose your friend Mary enjoys making fish chowder and puts in a lot of pepper to make it hot and spicy. Suppose also that you cannot enjoy chowder when it has that much pepper. Using the Seventh Pathway that advises you to communicate your feelings, you tell her that you cannot enjoy the chowder when it has so much pepper. Suppose Mary replies that it is better to put the pepper in when it is cooking so that it can become blended. If you work from the Power Level of Consciousness, you will get into an argument and point out that it tastes just about as good if the pepper is added later by each individual. Then Mary will mirror your annoyance—and soon love, peace, and serenity have temporarily departed. If Mary accepts your attempt to dominate the situation to fit your inside pattern, she may leave out the pepper but feel resentful towards you. You will have less pepper, but you may also have less love with your meal.

Now suppose you handle the problem of the pepper in the chowder with the complete knowledge that love and expanded consciousness are always enough. You have previously communicated your feelings about how the pepper keeps you from enjoying the chowder. If Mary serves the hot chowder again, your love and expanded consciousness may tell you that it is more flowing to test it with a single sip and then concentrate on enjoying the people, the salad, and everything else around you. Just steer your ship around the rock gently and lovingly.

Don't put out the vibration that you can't enjoy the chowder because of the pepper—for this would just be another method of expressing irritation. Completely accept the fact that you're not supposed to be eating chowder that night, and go ahead and enjoy whatever there is to enjoy. Don't put out any feeling tones that could make Mary uncomfortable because you are sacrificing yourself and not eating the chowder. Just flow as though the chowder had never been served.

If you can love Mary just as much when she does not follow your request to leave out the pepper, it is very likely that your love and expanded consciousness will enable you to enjoy unpeppered chowder the next time. For Mary is a conscious being, and she will notice that you are not eating the chowder. She will also notice your complete acceptance of this, and she will not be likely to get upset about it. She will just accept it as "that which is." Mary will appreciate your not complaining repeatedly about putting in too much pepper. She may begin to feel that although she prefers putting in the pepper when it is cooking, she has a greater preference for your enjoying the chowder next time. So you may find that Mary may quietly omit the pepper the next time she makes the chowder. If you can keep your consciousness completely free of the Power

Center, you will help Mary stay away from her Power Center. And the simple matter of peppering the chowder will not become complex because of the ego stuff that you mirror back and forth.

And what if Mary does not choose to make the chowder the next time with less pepper? You simply accept that as being a part of the here and nowness of your life. You're not supposed to be eating chowder when she fixes it. This is not a great sacrifice. You may not be enjoying chowder, but you are enjoying love and serenity—*which are far more nourishing than any chowder could ever be.* You are also helping Mary enjoy peace, love, and serenity and this is the greatest gift that you could give her. If you are addicted to chowder and have to eat it, you could always go out and buy a cup for lunch tomorrow. You will find that your love and increased consciousness will always give you the optimal ways to veer around problems or lovingly eliminate them.

Always remember that the individual with the higher consciousness is the one *who is most flexible*—who avoids fixed patterns—who flows in every life situation so as not to get involved in addictive irritations. The individual with the higher consciousness creates a peaceful world in which to live. This can be done regardless of whether or not you are with people who are consciously working on their growth. It takes two people to have an ego battle. *But it only takes one person to create the peace and love of higher consciousness!* The other person does not have to know the Living Love Way and does not have to be trying to reprogram his alienating addictions. He can be inflexible, power-oriented, ego-dominated, and hostile. If *you* can operate from the Love Level of Consciousness or any higher level, your love and your conscious perceptiveness will enable you to flow in every situation.

Once we see the possibility of living in a peaceful and loving world all of the time (regardless of *anything* people may do or say), we find that there are certain life situations that often flip us back into the power level of consciousness. For example, our power addictions may manifest themselves when we know we are right, but the other person stubbornly refuses to follow our instructions. We need to remind ourselves that getting irritated will only make the situation more complicated. Oftentimes we get annoyed when we are inconvenienced in some way by another person. We irritate ourselves when people do not follow agreed-upon rules or when someone is thoughtless. We often create resentment in ourselves when we're trying to explain about how we think and what we're trying to do—and other people do not seem to be interested. We irritate ourselves when we perceive that another person is deceptive or he or she lets us down in one way or another.

We may get irritated when someone tells us something we already know. Or perhaps we are meditating and we annoy ourselves when someone is not sensitive to our desire for silence. Or perhaps we are busy and someone is not aware of our inner flow when we are trying to finish a task. Or we have responsibilities and another person does not recognize that this is our province where we're entitled to make decisions.

Sometimes we irritate ourselves when we find that other people are impatient and want us to move faster than we are moving. Or perhaps someone repeatedly interrupts us. Sometimes we feel paranoid when someone does not return our friendliness. Some of the people in our lives will attack us with anger and hostility. And unless we are thoroughly able to operate our consciousness on the fourth level of unconditional love, we will immediately throw ourselves back into the power level and our response will mirror their uptightness.

It is necessary for you to tell yourself that you have been trying to handle these situations all of your life by using dominance, pecking-order forcefulness, emotional uptightness, barter, gifts, and other manipulative techniques. These power methods have not yet enabled you to create a fulfilled and beautiful life. Now it is time to switch over and use only love and expanded consciousness as your guides whenever the actions of people do not fit the programs that you have conditioned into your biocomputer.

You need to continually remind yourself that in none of the above situations can you justify yourself at any time in becoming angry, irritable, resentful, fearful, jealous, or anxious. You need to realize that such situations are part of the nowness of your life. *The* *game is to emotionally accept the unacceptable.* You are trying to liberate yourself from your addictive traps. So you use all of these experiences to grow in consciousness. If you do get trapped into unloving dualistic Power Level behavior, you just consciously see the drama for what it is—and you resolve not to get trapped again. If you stumble, just get up and go on. Don't become addicted to not stumbling. *Use each fall back to the Power Level as a gift from your life to help you become more conscious and accepting.*

The energy you put into your growth toward higher consciousness can be increased if you deeply realize the enormous price you are now paying for your lower consciousness addictions—a toll in lost happiness, lost peace, lost love, lost serenity, lost wisdom, and lost effectiveness. If you put half the energy into your consciousness growth *that you put into living out your programmed addictions,* you would soon begin to live in the warmth and beauty of higher consciousness.

The level of consciousness at which you operate determines what you notice and what you don't notice. Your programming influences whether you see it all clearly or see it through distorting ego filters—whether it grabs your consciousness or is simply seen clearly for what it is.

Love and peace are not only your goals—they are also the methods you use to get to the goals. Always realize that it is only the programming in *your* head that is separating you from the beautiful feelings of higher consciousness every second of your life. Happiness is there waiting inside of you—and it becomes more available every time you reprogram one of your addictions.

20 Living Love with Children

A child can be a great teacher in your journey toward higher consciousness. A young child can give you a continuous demonstration of what it is like to live in the here and now before the rational mind affects the stream of consciousness. A child can turn its consciousness fully and spontaneously to each new life situation. When denied something that it wants, it may respond with an ego trip by crying. But one minute later, it can turn its attention to the here-and-now situation that life offers and be joyous and laughing again. Thus the conciousness of an infant does not grasp situations and churn them with the rational mind.

Children are very sensitive mirrors of your consciousness level. When they are surrounded by peaceful, loving people, they reflect a warm, flowing state most of the time. When they are surrounded by driven, other-directed, manipulating people, they rapidly reflect this tension and uptightness in their behavior.

Your level of consciousness determines your world. If you live in a world of fears and anxiety, you will pull the lower consciousness people around you into your psychic space. If your consciousness largely operates on the Power Center, any child with whom you continually interact will be pulled into your subject-object type of non-caring manipulations. If your responses to your child continually show loving thoughtfulness and acceptance of your child as an individual, this will be reflected in the child's consciousness.

Your head creates your child. If you view your child as awkward, you will create an awkward child. If you view your child as an interference to your important daily activities, you will create exactly this type of child. The images and classifications through which you perceive a child will be sensitively picked up by the child and *will play a large part in how he reacts to you.*

The people who interact continually with a young child determine the nature and strength of the future addictions that he or she must uplevel to preferences to grow into higher consciousness. When a child is around highly dominating people, a large portion of his energy will remain preoccupied with the Power Center of Consciousness. Upon reaching maturity, the adult will regard power as the key to happiness in the world. The child will have been bruised by uncaring, "Shut up, be quiet, and do exactly as I say" subject-object manipulation. The child will feel that happiness correlates with the amount of personal power and prestige one can use to dominate and control the people and situations in one's life. A child who is around flowing, higher consciousness people (who regard the child's needs as they would their own) will easily grow into the Love Center of Consciousness. With coming adulthood, he or she will have a life style that is characterized by harmoniously flowing with the here-and-now situations of life. *The child will know deep in his or her being that love and expanded consciousness will always bring whatever is needed for happiness.*

If you observe the interaction between most adults and children from the point of view of the Security Center, Sensation Center, and Power Center of Consciousness, you will feel compassion for the robot-like behavior that has ensnared both the child and the adult. The consciousness of the adult will tend to magnify most of the actions of the child as threats to the adult's security, sensation, or power. Since children mirror our consciousness, this leads the child to develop strong addictive programming on the first three levels. The developing being will have heavy psychological obstacles that must be reprogrammed to permit growth into the Love Center and Cornucopia Center. No one can progress to these higher centers as long as he or she feels that happiness is just a matter of having enough security, sex, money, prestige, and power!

We create security, sensation, and power addictions in children when we try to dominate them with such emotional demands as, "I've told you a thousand times to. . . . What is the matter with you? . . . . Don't you ever listen? . . . . I've never seen a dumber . . . . For the last time, I want you to get this straight. . . . Just do that once more and. . . ." As Dr. Haim Ginott says, "Our 'normal' talk drives children crazy: the blaming and shaming, preaching and moralizing, accusing and guilt-giving, ridiculing and belittling, threatening and bribing, evaluating and labeling." Watch how *you* feel when people talk to you in such heavily dualistic ways.

We should replace our alienating, criticizing words with "I" language. Instead of, "You are a liar and no one can trust you," say, "I don't like it when I can't rely on your words—it is difficult for us to do things together." *You talk only about your exact feelings here and now.* You don't chew over the past or threaten future punishments. You skip the disparaging pseudo-analysis of the child's character based on your addictive ego demands.

How do you use the experience of being with a child to aid you in your growth toward higher consciousness? The child can help you develop an awareness of what an "unfurnished" mind is like. When a child is first born, he does not chew over situations with his rational mind. He is just totally right here—right now. You can observe in a very young infant some (but definitely not all) of the characteristics of higher consciousness. A child is usually very perceptive in picking up the true feelings and vibrations of those around him. The nervous system of a young child is heavily programmed for crying and other emotional behaviors that can dominate the consciousness of adults within earshot so that they will be aware of his or her needs. As fellow travelers on the road to higher consciousness, we should see our adult roles as loving and serving every child. This helps the child to make a rapid transition from crying and other emotional behavior to a programming that permits meeting needs through love and expanded consciousness.

The creation of a heaven on earth in which everyone lives in a world free of wars, misunderstanding, and duality on every level requires that we no longer train our children to develop intense security, sensation, and power addictions. It is easy to blame the problems of the world on governments, schools, and uncaring economic institutions, but this is only an evasion. *All of these institutions are us.* The non-loving, subject-object actions of all of these institutions have been created and are maintained by addictions that we have acquired. Even the polarity of our addictive opposition may strengthen what we may wish to change!

The only effective and permanent way to change the world in which we live is to change our level of consciousness. And one of the best ways to repair the strong addictive programming that has been conditioned into our biocomputer is to interact with children. We can save them from the suffering that would await them if they were to develop heavily programmed power addictions and demands. In return, we will benefit by being reminded of what it is like to live in the here and now, to enjoy a consciousness that is not continually churned up by the rational mind, and to benefit by the mirror which the child provides to enable us to see our own addictions.

Your life will give you continual opportunities to show the child (and yourself) whether you are on a power level of consciousness or a love level of consciousness. Every glass of milk that the child spills enables you to show him the world in which your Conscious-awareness lives. Do you say (or even *silently feel*), "I've told you a thousand times to be more careful. The next time you spill a glass of milk you are going to stand in the corner for one hour. I'm sick and tired of your clumsy carelessness. It's about time you listened to me. Why don't you get that rag and clean it up? Are you helpless?" If so, you will be training the child to dominate his consciousness by security, sensation, and power addictions. And since your consciousness creates your universe through these filters, you will live in a subject-object world in which your inner serenity is constantly threatened by the acts of the child. You are simply using the spilled milk to create heavier and heavier low-consciousness programming *for both of you.* And a low-consciousness life is full of spilled milk—in one form or another.

When a child spills the milk, *you could welcome it as an op-*

portunity to help both of you grow into higher consciousness. You can say to yourself, "The milk is spilled—right here, right now. Fussing about it won't unspill the milk. It will simply irritate both myself and the child. An upset child may unconsciously knock over another glass. I've knocked over glasses hundreds of times. This is just a normal part of living. The immature muscle control of a child increases the probability of spilled milk. But even now as an adult I sometimes spill things. So we're losing a few ounces of milk, but that's absolutely no reason to lose our love and serenity." And you keep on talking about whatever you were saying before the milk was spilled. It should be cleaned up *as a usual thing to do.* You don't need to head-trip the child by saying such things as, "That's all right, everybody spills milk," unless the feelings of the child call for further words. *You convey those thoughts by your loving, flowing acceptance of the spilled milk and your simple, natural cleaning-up actions.*

After spilling the milk, the child will be very sensitive to your feelings and will pick up any paranoia or antagonism in your consciousness—even though you may be very sweet and tactful in your words. If you can *really* accept the spilled milk (as well as other non-preferred happenings in your life) and permit your consciousness to flow in a here-and-now loving way, there will be very little "spilled milk" in your life. But if your consciousness gets caught up in one incident after another that involves your security, sensation, or power programming, you can create a living hell in your daily interaction with a child.

The Twelve Pathways presented in Chapter 4 should be memorized so that you can get them below your rational level into the deeper circuitry of your biocomputer that controls how you see your world. These Twelve Pathways show you the road to higher consciousness. Whenever you are angry, fearful, or jealous, you will find that it is because you have ignored one or more of the Pathways. While they apply to every situation in your life, it is especially important that you use them when interacting with children. You are giving them *models of programming* that they will duplicate to "make it" in life.

Children will rapidly integrate the challenges of life when they are around adults who openly communicate from the Fourth or higher Centers of Consciousness. The Seventh Pathway says, "I open myself genuinely to all people by being willing to fully communicate my deepest feelings, since hiding in any degree keeps me stuck in my illusion of separateness from other people." This is especially important with children, for their ability to tune in to you on the feeling level is very accurate. If you feel one thing and say something else, you will be training them in dishonesty. Even though their rational minds may not yet permit them to be as adept at word games as you are, their relative freedom from rationality makes them more perceptive of feelings even though you cleverly manipulate them with words. Children intuitively sense your dishonesty and will not trust you. However, they will mirror your conduct by learning to manipulate *you* with words. When you label and criticize them, they will mirror this by labeling and criticizing *you*. When you threaten and bribe them, they will threaten and bribe *you*. And they can often beat you at mirroring your games!

Always remember that everything that makes you upset in your interactions with a child represents **your addictions—not his.** When your addictive programming makes you upset, you will respond to a child in a way that helps to program addictions into his biocomputer. When you respond to every here-and-now situation in a loving, conscious way, you will be able to do exactly what needs to be done. The Ninth Pathway is very helpful, "I act freely when I am tuned in, centered, and loving, but if possible I avoid acting when I am emotionally upset and depriving myself of the wisdom that flows from love and expanded consciousness."

Although you will find all of the Pathways useful when living with children, the Twelfth Pathway should be particularly uppermost in your consciousness: "I am perceiving everyone, including myself, as an awakening being who is here to claim his or her birthright to the higher consciousness planes of unconditional love and oneness." How do you treat an awakening being? Do you criticize him, belittle him, evaluate him, bribe him, get angry with him, try to manipulate him? Or do you just love him and serve him? If he asks you to do something, you do it if you are able to. If you cannot do it, you know that he will understand. Children have a deep understanding on intuitive levels. If their consciousness has not been muddied with power games, children are very realistic in accepting the here and now conditions in their lives.

The Living Love Catalyst, ALL WAYS US LIVING LOVE, (See the Fourth Method in Chapter 13) can be helpful in freeing your consciousness from security, sensation, and power addictions when interacting with children. You may wish to start this Catalyst in your consciousness and keep it going for many hours. You let words and other sounds, visual impulses, and touch sensations pour into the background of your consciousness. When you keep ALL WAYS US LIVING LOVE constantly turning in your mind, your vibrations will become more peaceful and loving. The perceptions which are then placed into your Conscious-awareness by your vast and complex biocomputer will be those which tune you in to a deep calm place within yourself and the children around you. Since children are such excellent mirrors, anything you do to uplevel your consciousness will rapidly be reflected in an upleveling of the consciousness of the children around you.

Unless you are free of the lower three levels of consciousness, from time to time your addictive emotional programming will fill your consciousness with fear, anger, or resentment. When this happens, you use these emotional feelings as a golden opportunity to reprogram yourself through the Method of Consciousness Focusing. This is the Fifth Method of growth in the Living Love Way to Higher Consciousness. If you constantly use the here-and-now experience that your life is giving you, your interaction with children can rapidly accelerate your growth into higher consciousness. You should regard it as an evasion if you tell yourself that you cannot grow into higher consciousness because you have young children to take care of—and they are such a distraction. It is likely that you can grow into higher consciousness *more rapidly because you do have the benefit of interacting with children.*

Firmness is sometimes necessary in order to teach a child how to live with others and to cope with the physical dangers of the world. One mother might punish a child from a subject-object, alienated space that will create separation. Another mother may "punish" a child in the same way but from a Fourth Center, loving space that will bring them closer together. *The things that you actually do in interacting with a child are not as important as the Center of Consciousness that you are working from.* A person at the Fourth Center of Consciousness prefers to be receptive and accepting, but when life requires it, he or she can use firmness or force from a loving space. Parents operating from the Fourth Center of Consciousness will do what needs to be done in each situation—and accept and love both the child and themselves—seeing it all as part of the warp and woof of the universe.

Always remember that the experience of peace, love, and serenity are created by the way in which *you* operate *your* biocomputer. The world you perceive is based on the automatic programming below conscious levels that selects everything that is introduced into your consciousness. As you grow into higher consciousness, your perceptions of what is here and now in your life will be introduced into your consciousness without triggering emotions that lead your rational mind to churn away with security, sensation, and power stuff. When a panoramic perception of the here and now is introduced into your consciousness within a framework of openness and love, you live in a deep, calm place within your heart. You will perceive the drama going on outside of you. You will effectively do what you need to do. And *you will enjoy as drama* all of the "ugly" things and the "beautiful" things that are being acted out on the stage that passes before your eyes each day. The joy and ecstasy of life is yours as you become one with the Law of Higher Consciousness—**Love everyone unconditionally—including yourself.**

21
HOW TO INCREASE YOUR ENJOYMENT OF SEX

Sex, as well as the rest of the drama in your life, may be experienced at any level of consciousness. It may be done on the security level (as in the case of a turned-off wife who lets it happen to keep her marriage together), on the sensation level (as with a playboy), or on the power level (such as a man who challenges himself to make it with a difficult-to-get partner). Sex is experienced on the love level of consciousness (when you use the experience to flow more lovingly and acceptingly), or on the Cornucopia level (when one finds in the experience of sex a deeper awareness of the way in which life offers us everything we need). On the sixth level of consciousness one watches the drama of the physical union from a deep calm place within one's heart. On the seventh level of consciousness, one becomes the sexual experience. It is not perceived as something that is happening to oneself. Instead, one feels an identity with everything and everyone. On this level, you would not *experience* sex as a happening—you are the happening. . . .

Unless you are well on your way on the journey to higher consciousness, you are probably now experiencing sex largely on the second level of consciousness. You engage in sex with your partner for your mutual enjoyment. Your consciousness during sex is concerned with the sensations that you have during the time you are making love—and especially during the moments of orgasm. The consciousness of your partner similarly will be focused on the delightful sensations. Although there is cooperation and agreement between you regarding what is happening, each of you *is using the other as an object* with which to gratify a desire for sexual feelings. There is thus a subject-object separateness that deprives you of the more beautiful feelings that await you when sex is experienced from higher levels of consciousness.

Sex at the second level of consciousness leaves you vulnerable in many ways. You may compare tonight's experience with the high feelings of a previous night, and this comparison may lead you to feel that what happened tonight was not quite "enough." You are vulnerable to disappointment if your partner is tired or for some reason is not interested. If the experience is particularly great, your consciousness will begin to wonder how soon you can repeat it—or whether you can repeat it at all.

This grasping, manipulative focus of consciousness keeps you from being completely satisfied here and now. It keeps you on a roller-coaster of pleasure and disappointment. Our habit of anticipating the future rather than letting ourselves completely experience the here-and-now enjoyment of life can enormously detract from the experience of sex. For example, a man may spend an evening dining and talking with a woman with a large proportion of his consciousness involved in his anticipation of going to bed with her later that night. He is bodily with her, but a large part of his consciousness is drained away by his preoccupation with the future. If the person he is with is perceptive (and not caught in the same game), she will be aware that there is something lacking in the vividness and oneness of their here-and-now interactions.

Let us suppose his plan works out, and they are now in bed kissing each other. The man's consciousness (if he has not learned how to be in the here and now) will not be totally enjoying the experience of kissing. He will be anticipating the next step when perhaps his hands will be caressing her breasts. Once he is caressing her breasts, he is very likely to miss the "enoughness" and delightfulness of *that* experience. He will be anticipating how nice it will be when his hands begin to explore yet more intimate regions that await him below her hips. And then when he is next touching and feeling her labial and vaginal areas, he will still not be here now. He will still be unable to savor and completely appreciate the nowness of the experience. His consciousness will then leap forward to anticipate how nice it will be when his penis is inside of her. And even after that happens, he may still not be in the here and now! He will be anticipating the moments of climax. It is only when he finally reaches orgasm that he will be completely here now. For the moments of orgasm are so consciousness-dominating that he will probably not be able to place his consciousness anywhere else. It is one of the few times in his life when he can experience being completely in the here and now!

When your consciousness is dominated by your desire for the intense sensations of sex, you will be depriving yourself of a large part of the beauty and loveliness that will be yours when you can enjoy sex at the Fourth Center of Consciousness. When your consciousness is operating at the Fourth Level, you will begin to enjoy every second as a fulfilling whole in itself. *Whatever happens as the flow of love unfolds is enough.* Your mind is not concerned with what will be happening a few seconds or a few minutes from now. Hence, it is not grasping. It is not manipulating. It is not striving. It is not comparing. It is not trying to make anything happen. It is just flowing completely with your feelings and the feelings of your partner—and the nowness of the environment around you.

If you would like to know whether your consciousness is dominated by sex, you might apply the following test. You can probably do this in your head. Suppose you have been in bed with your partner for a half-hour and are getting near the point where intercourse may begin. Then suppose your best friend knocks on the door. He has a serious problem and it is urgent that he see you immediately. Can you without disappointment—without any grasping at the previous experience—let your consciousness flow to this new here-and-now situation in your life? Can you turn to this new situation without irritability, anger, or disappointment of any sort? Can you rechannel that energy that was created by lovemaking into helping your friend? If your consciousness can flow from one here-and-now experience to the next here-and-now experience, you are peacefully and beautifully flowing in the river of your life.

An individual who is hung up on the second level of consciousness will irritate himself, his sexual partner, and his friend in the situation described above. Once he has talked with his friend and done whatever is necessary, his consciousness will still be clouded by resentment toward what he perceives as an intrusion. When he then returns to be with his lover, his consciousness will be preoccupied with the immediate past. Instead of flowingly enjoying the here and now when uninterrupted sex is possible, his preoccupation with the past may keep him from doing that which he most wants to do!

An individual who is hung up on the second level of consciousness can never live completely in the here and now. For example, a woman who is addicted at the second level will scan everyone she sees as a sexual partner. Her response to all of the beautiful individuals who flow into her life will be limited by her analysis of whether this person would fit the pattern in her head that she has for an exciting bed partner. Instead of reacting to the whole person in front of her, she is only tuning in to a very small slice of what is available. She is depriving herself of the broad spectrum that life is offering her. She is disregarding the Second Pathway by creating an illusory version of the people around her. It is the opposite of the openness which brings the miracle of "enoughness" into one's life.

A person whose consciousness is dominated by sex may be led to purchase automobiles, homes, clothes, boats, and most of the things in his or her life on a basis of their supposed contribution to future sexual experiences. The things purchased may be too costly, not wear well, or may have many other disadvantages. If they are too expensive, they will put a person in debt or cause him to focus more of his consciousness on earning money. This has the repercussion of taking time and energy away from sexual activities that one tells oneself will bring pleasure. It is thus with all addictive patterns which keep us on the self-defeating pursuit of illusory concepts of fulfillment and happiness.

What do we do when we discover that a large part of our consciousness is trapped on the second level? The Third Method for consciousness growth, explained in Chapter 13, can be helpful in enabling us to reprogram this addiction. Sexual addictions can gradually wear away when we become consciously aware of the resultant disadvantages and suffering that an addiction causes. Our growing insight reveals the penalties we are unnecessarily paying: the way we alienate people we would like to love because of the intrusiveness of our subject-object manipulation, the disappointment, irritation, and anger that a sexual addiction can trigger, the drain on our pocketbooks, the anxiety that we experience if we have a model for always reaching orgasm, etc.

The addiction to sex can be so powerful that it may help if you stop your usual sexual dance for a period of time in order to give you a chance to permit other patterns to emerge. For example, if you definitely resolve not to have sex for the next three months, you may help your consciousness to get free of domination by sex thoughts and addictions. This can liberate your consciousness to tune in to him or her without any overtones of "Let's go to bed tonight." This may broaden your activities together. It can increase your openness to more fully experiencing the person as a human being. You will begin to free yourself from the diminished awareness that occurs when your consciousness is focused on sexual interactions.

During this temporary moratorium on sex, you can focus your consciousness on fully enjoying every here-and-now experience. You may wish to enjoy just massaging each other. Since your consciousness will not be preoccupied with making anything happen beyond the massage, you can both be completely free to thoroughly experience the here and nowness of the massage. You are consciously reprogramming yourself to become non-addicted to the experience of orgasm. You begin to realize that this ten-second orgasm that sex offers can dominate too large a part of your Conscious-awareness. It gives a hollowness to hours and hours of your precious consciousness—keeping you out of the here and now—and making you unable to fully tune in to the full reality that is available to you every moment of your life. You begin to see that

The past
is dead
The future
is imaginary
Happiness
can only be
in the Eternal
Now
Moment

the experience of orgasm is not worth the many hours per day during which it may deprive you of tuning in to everything around you through multichannel perception.

But a beautiful thing about consciousness growth is that *when you give it up, you get it all back.* For you are not training yourself to *reject* orgasm—that would be substituting one addiction for another. *That which you emotionally reject is also an addiction that will bring unhappiness.* You're simply training yourself to let the experience of orgasm be part of the enjoyable nowness of your life. When you can let sex *flow into your life* as part of the *spontaneous unfoldment* of the situations that life offers you, your life will probably bring you more satisfying sexual experiences than you ever had before. And these experiences will be without the disadvantages of having your consciousness dominated with striving to achieve them. You can then enjoy sex (or anything else) without paying a heavy price in lowered perceptions and disappointments.

Suppose you have successfully placed a moratorium on sex for whatever period you need to reprogram your consciousness so that you can become free of the second level. Let us suppose that you have begun to interact with a sexual partner on a broader, nonsexual basis. You will find yourself enjoying simple things together that before would have been boring—or at best tolerated as a stepping stone to getting into bed. You begin to experience more deeply the inner beauty of the human being that you are with. You experience him or her on a deeper level of being. Your consciousness is freed from responding as though he or she is an object for your sexual enjoyment.

You may then choose to begin sexual activities but limit them for a few nights to playful interactions that create a sensitive intimacy—perhaps just caressing and exploring one another's bodies without going as far as a climax. The reason for doing this is to experience the *enoughness* of whatever you are doing. You will discover that when you are completely tuned in and loving, it is absolutely enough *just to be with a person.* Whatever you *do* can be experienced as "enough" if you are not trying to make something happen—or trying to keep something from happening. Focus your consciousness on the full enjoyment of the nowness between you and your partner. Learn to let each moment flow from the previous one without planning, pushing, or trying to control the flow of one moment into another.

Become completely sensitive to every nuance of your partner. Your verbal and non-verbal communication should be so effective that you know whether your partner is enjoying the flow of events. The cues you need are there—you only need to let them into your consciousness. *It should never be necessary for him or her to reject an insensitive action.* This is oneness. This delicate beauty of the here and now can only be found when you and your partner flow as one consciousness.

You do not have to strive for or reject any particular sexual positions—it is all beautiful. Where your body is and what it is doing are not vital—where your consciousness operates is completely vital. As long as there is a oneness flowing between you and your partner, any sexual activities may be enjoyed as part of the drama. *Each moment is prized for itself and is not experienced as a stepping stone to what will happen next.*

To experience your sexual partner on the fourth level of consciousness, you may wish to begin the sexual dance by sitting facing each other and looking into each other's eyes. This should be enough—just to look into the eyes of your beloved without any need to touch or do anything else. Do not focus on his or her eyes for this can produce ego personality games. Instead let your gaze rest gently on the bridge of the nose directly between the eyes. You will usually notice a light spot where the nose joins the forehead. *Search for this circle of light and hold onto it.* You will still see the eyes, the nose, the lips—the entire face. The face of your partner will assume many forms and shapes. You will see him or her in ways that you have never experienced before—both ugly and beautiful. But do not hold onto any of these perceptions. Let them pass as part of the dance of life. Let your love, acceptance, and oneness grow as you just sit there looking into the face of your beloved. Continue this until you find it completely enough—until you experience that your mind is emptied of restless designs and nothing more is desired. You may wish to start the phrase ALL WAYS US LIVING LOVE to add to the beauty you are creating.

Then as love and oneness grow, other things may just happen by themselves. You may find that you get into a position where the man is lying on his back with the woman sitting astride on top facing him. This is known as the Maithuna position in the ancient Eastern science of Tantric yoga. In this position you can gaze into each other's eyes, your hands can touch each other and caress a large part of each other's body. When the woman is sitting on top she is able to sensitively modulate the degree of stimulation during intercourse so that arousal proceeds in a mutually heightening way. Perhaps you may sometimes wish to enjoy this position for an hour or more with your partner without reaching a climax. This will free your consciousness of the expectation of something that is to happen in the future. It will enable you to completely enjoy every part of the here-and-now experience that life is offering you.

On the fourth level of consciousness, sex is sought as a way of growing in love and oneness. When your consciousness is no longer focused on an addictive demand for sex, the exquisite sensations are still there and they are more fully and consistently enjoyed. You are now completely free from all vulnerability to grasping or disappointment. You can flow with whatever happens. You can completely enjoy each moment for itself.

This growth will open the doors to your enjoying sex on a higher level of consciousness. On the fifth level, you become more aware that life is boundlessly generous in sending you everything you need for happiness—*even more than you can possibly need.* You realize that it gave you second level happenings which enabled you to experience disappointment and suffering in your sexual activities so that you could grow to higher levels. You now realize that the irritations you felt when someone did not go to bed with you (or when things did not happen as you had planned when you did go to bed) were given to you by your life to help you grow into higher consciousness. You now see that every sexual experience has helped to set the stage for your present growth into higher consciousness.

So you learn to use sex (as well as everything else you do in your daily life) to accelerate you on your journey into higher consciousness. You realize that your mind creates the world in which you live. Your mind puts you in different places and leads you to experience different things to help you grow in consciousness. You see the sexual dance as part of the drama of your life and you know that when you are open, accepting, and loving, you will experience the optimal happiness that awaits you.*

* ***A Conscious Person's Guide to Relationships*** **by Ken Keyes, Jr. offers practical Living Love guidelines on preparing for a relationship and getting the most out of your relationship. See Appendix 5 for more information.**

22
THE OPTIMAL USE OF YOUR BIOCOMPUTER

The human biocomputer (or brain) is a fantastically sensitive instrument with enormous capabilities. But like any complex tool, it cannot be used optimally unless cautions and training are given to the user. We can easily be misled into the illusion that our consciousness is aware of what is really happening both inside our biocomputer and in the outside world of our body and the people and things around us.

Our consciousness is somewhat like the president of a large business who has information on a small part of the space-time events that are going on in the many offices and factories of the corporation. The president receives *preprocessed abstracted information*. Normally, *he works from abstractions of abstractions.* It is therefore most important that he be conscious of this abstracting process. Similarly, you and I, as users of our magnificent biocomputers, should realize that our consciousness can only be aware of perhaps one-millionth of the incoming information each second of the day. Every hair on our body is connected with our biocomputer. All of our internal organs are constantly sending information to and receiving information from our great biocomputer—usually on levels below our consciousness. Our receptor organs of sight, sound, touch, taste, and smell, plus the kinesthetic senses which give information regarding our body are continually sending in millions of impulses per second toward our biocomputer. The eye alone is connected to the biocomputer with over two million nerve fibers. The ears are connected to the biocomputer by over a hundred thousand nerves. This tremendous mass of data going into our biocomputer second by second would be absolutely overwhelming if it were not for the *underlying systems of organization that automatically abstract, classify, suppress, or distribute this huge flood of incoming sensory information. Our consciousness operates on preprocessed, filtered abstractions of abstractions received from various parts of our biocomputer.*

THE ABSTRACTING PROCESS

Our universe is made up of matter and energy. Every material object is composed of atoms, which in turn are made up of even finer subatomic particles such as electrons. These are in an incessant state of zizzy-fast motion. Atoms group together to form molecules, which are still too fine to be registered by our five senses unless special instruments, such as an electron microscope, are used. The smooth table that I experience with my fingers is an abstraction from the table on the atomic level that is composed of flying atoms. A characteristic of the abstracting process is *that some aspects are left out each time there is an abstraction.* When our senses report the smoothness of a table, obviously a fantastic number of characteristics are left out. Our senses "manufacture" a smooth sensation by abstracting from the colloidal, molecular, atomic, and subatomic activity that lies behind the object reported by our sensory equipment.

Our senses do not permit us to tune in to reality—they only pick up that small aspect of reality that is transmittable through electromagnetic waves. Further abstractions take place when these are projected by the lenses of our eyes onto our retinas and transformed again into electrochemical impulses that proliferate throughout our brains. As the circuits of our biocomputer are activated by the huge stream of incoming electrical impulses, even more abstracting takes place. The tiny portion selected for projection onto the screen of our consciousness represents a highly processed abstraction of an abstraction of an abstraction, etc.

Our senses and our rational mind do not tune in to the world as it is. The picture of the world that comes into our consciousness is mostly a creation of the human biocomputer with its vast memory bank and distorting addictive programming. These processed products that reach our consciousness reflect the limitations and idiosyncrasies of our biocomputer and the programming from which it operates—just as much as they reflect the outside energies that spark the process. The part that a hen plays in the production of an omelette is analogous to the part the outside world plays in producing the stuff that is projected onto the screen of our consciousness. When we realize how our minds manipulate, suppress, change, and distort, *we begin to perceive the awesome way in which our heads create our world.*

Although the human biocomputer works as an integrated system, it is possible to point out certain neural structures that are especially important to the student of human consciousness. These are:

1. The Cerebral Cortex

The cerebral cortex is a thin outer covering of the side and upper parts of the convoluted surfaces of the brain which has from ten billion to thirteen billion cortical cells. These brain cells and their connections are the structures that enable our remarkable rational mind to be aware of being aware, to use words and symbols, and to comprehend complex systems of thought, such as mathematics, science, and art. Generally, other animals have only a fraction of the cortical cells that are our birthright as human beings.

Although we possess this remarkable equipment, we are not automatically experts in how to use it. Special training (such as the instructions contained in this book) are required to operate in the higher states of consciousness which represent the optimal functioning of our human biocomputer.

Unless you have freed your biocomputer from consciousness-dominating addictions and demands, your cerebral cortex will

The Human Biocomputer

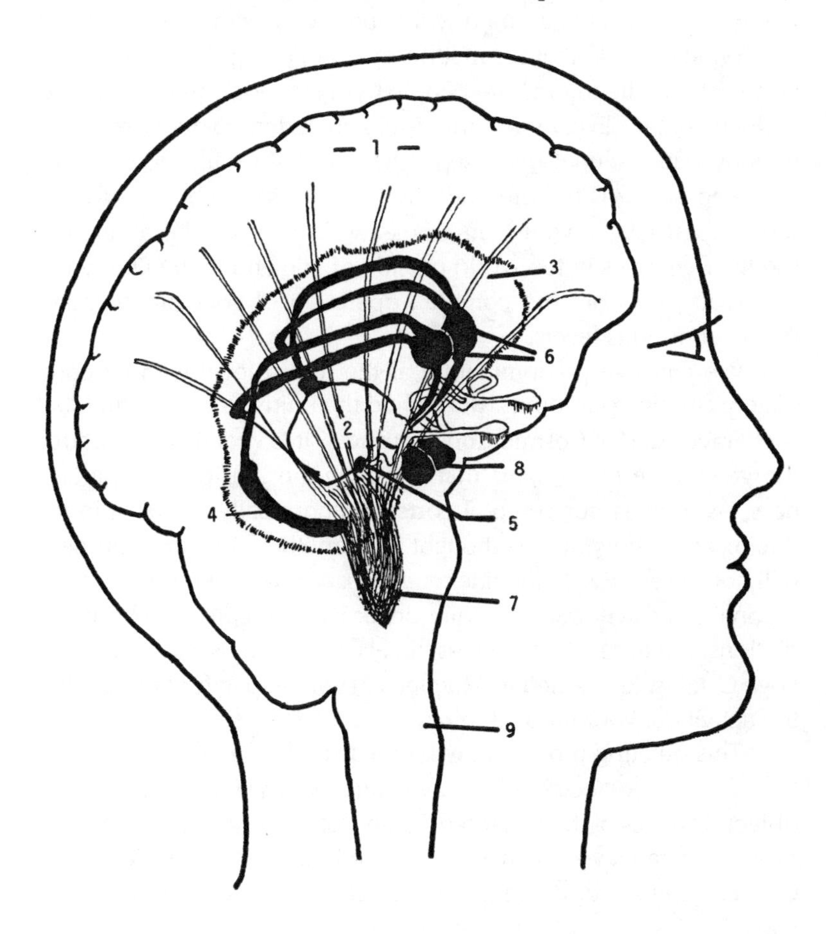

1. Cortex
2. Thalamus
3. Limbic Lobes
4. Hippocampus
5. Amygdala
6. Septal Region
7. Reticular Activating System
8. Hypothalamic Nuclei
9. Brain Stem

continually chew over a situation in which you do not have what you want. Your rational mind will churn away with such questions as, "What did I do that resulted in my not getting this? What can I do to get it in the future? Are people trying to block me? Do people really like me?" Every word that is channeled into your consciousness by your rational mind separates you by a milli-second from the deepest levels of here-and-now awareness. To be sensitive to the deepest levels, your Conscious-awareness must be attuned to the finer energies in the world outside of you and to the finer energies that arise from the complex operation of your biocomputer below conscious levels.

We can live predominantly at the fourth level without completely calming our minds. But to find the unitive state of mind that is characteristic of Cosmic Consciousness, it is vital that we control the generation of thoughts that continue the illusion of separateness. As long as our cerebral cortex is continually active in introducing and following one thought after another, our consciousness will not be sensitive to the finer energies. A degree of quieting of the rational mind will automatically occur as you reprogram your addictions. But to reach the highest levels of consciousness, the Living Love Catalyst (explained in Chapter 13) will help in further quieting the activity of your rational mind.

This quieting process may be measured by an electroencephalograph that detects alpha waves and beta waves. The subject-object activities of the first three Centers of Consciousness generally produce beta waves. As we go into the Fourth and Fifth Centers of Consciousness, our cerebral cortex begins to produce more alpha waves.

2. The Limbic System

One of the underlying processing systems of the brain is the limbic system that plays a paramount part in the generation of emotional feelings. One of its major functions is to compare the incoming stimuli from the body and the sensory receptors with the programmed instructions that have been put into it by our experiences to date. The limbic system interacts with the cerebral cortex to pick up perceptions and memories, and to use the facilities of the cortex for analyzing such data. The hippocampus (which is part of the limbic system) plays a part in evaluating the incoming stimuli in terms of one's past experiences.

The amygdala (another component of the limbic system) functions to *intensify an emotional response whenever the incoming stimuli do not fit the expected patterns.* In other words, whenever anything *new and unexpected* happens, the amygdala may immediately begin to generate an emotional reaction such as anxiety, fear, anger, etc. It will send out impulses which travel through the thalamic area and trigger the release of hormones that cause you to feel upset, increase the adrenalin in your blood, speed up your heart rate, increase your blood sugar, and do other things to prepare you for a fight or flight reaction.

Another part of the limbic system is the septal region which plays a part in toning down our emotional reactions. The activation of this system helps to release us from emotional tension. All of the Five Consciousness Growth Methods are designed to enable you to activate the septal area. When you consciously place your attention on finding the most appropriate method to use in each situation, you reinforce the functioning of the septal region. This results in rapidly quieting uptight feelings, calming the pounding heart, and reducing the flow of adrenalin pouring into the bloodstream.

The biological function of the limbic system was *to help our ancestors survive the perils of the jungle.* This system that controls emotional feelings does everything it can (by enticing us with pleasure or forcing us through fear or anger) to make us follow the programming we have put into it. These emotional feelings act as dominating, sharp-pointed prods to make us do that which we have associated in the past (whether correctly or incorrectly) with our happiness, safety, and emotional well-being.

Unfortunately, most of the programming that directs the activity of our emotions consists of antiquated patterns that we programmed during infancy and early childhood when we were not sufficiently conscious to clearly evaluate the addictions of our parents, teachers, etc. Because of these low-consciousness instructions still resident in our biocomputers, in most social situations we end up doing that which violates our best psychosomatic interests, our real safety, and our genuine happiness.

Thus the limbic system operates below the level of consciousness as directed by our programmed addictions. Our consciousness usually becomes aware of fear, jealousy, anger, etc., *after* these emotional backups of our addictions have been initiated. We respond to words and personality interactions as though they were tigers about to devour us. Until we train ourselves in the optimal use of our biocomputer, our Conscious-awareness remains a captive audience of our low-level security, sensation, and power programming.

3. The Reticular Activating System

Another part of our biocomputer of paramount interest to the student of consciousness is the reticular activating system (RAS). Our understanding of the vital functions of the RAS is based on new research within the past decade. Anatomically, the RAS is a cone-shaped complex of nerves radiating from the brain stem. The nerve fibers of the RAS filter incoming sensory information and determine whether it is to be a part of *the very tiny trickle of information* that is permitted into our precious consciousness. The RAS is one of the brain's most important action systems for it literally functions as the "doorkeeper" to our consciousness.

The activities of the RAS have traditionally been referred to by the term "ego." This is the mechanism that uses your emotions *as pleasure-pain whips that force you to guard your security, sensation, and power addictions* (and even subtler ones) and continually direct your energy toward enhancing them. The RAS decides from one moment to the next what incoming sensory information, if any, shall be reported to your consciousness. The RAS can put you to sleep or it can wake you up. If your consciousness is deeply occupied, the RAS can shut off incoming stimuli so that you can concentrate. Even as you read these words, your RAS is probably blocking out auditory sensations so that you are not aware of sounds around you, and has probably been suppressing information on whether your body is comfortable so as to permit you to keep your attention on this book. However, your RAS is programmed to override your concentration on the book so that it will immediately pass on to you the fact that someone just entered the room and mentioned your name.

Your RAS interacting with your programming determines the world you perceive. You do not see the world as it is—you overemphasize the small slice of the world that resonates with your fears, desires, demands, hopes, and expectations. As you grow into higher consciousness, your RAS will interact with love and acceptance programming, and then **your love will create your world.** You will see everything (both the dualistic and the non-dualistic) as a manifestation of the energy of love. When your RAS is programmed to emphasize the Fifth Center of Consciousness, it will permit you to experience the world as an intricately beautiful complex of here and now energies that give you everything you need for evolving into a fully conscious being.

The RAS does not analyze or interpret incoming information. It works on the basis of the strength of the electrochemical impulse and whether the nerve impulses fit programmed patterns. For example, if you live next to a railroad track, your RAS has been so conditioned that it does not regard a thundering, house-shaking series of sounds as unusual while you are asleep. For someone whose RAS has not been trained in this manner, these sounds would cause the RAS to immediately awaken the individual and dominate his consciousness with the thundering clatter—to say nothing of repercussions in the limbic area!

The RAS maintains a two-way exchange of information with the cortex. As the doorkeeper to our consciousness, the RAS is affected by what is going on in our consciousness as well as playing a paramount part in determining what is introduced into our consciousness. When we operate on lower-consciousness levels, the

You make
yourself and
others suffer
just as much
when

you take offense

as when

you give
offense

RAS acts somewhat like the President of a country during a war. The information that is most likely to dominate his consciousness involves military matters. When we operate on low-consciousness levels, the RAS is most likely to pass on to our consciousness such "military matters" as security, sensations, and power. When peace comes, the President can give his attention to all aspects of the country. His consciousness is no longer dominated by the urgent "survival-threatening" war communiques.

To use our great biocomputer optimally, it is necessary for us to repeatedly and definitely give instructions to ourselves to eliminate the old programming and to replace it with *non-addictive preferential programming.* As this new Living Love programming begins to feed into the operation of our biocomputer, it relieves the RAS of the dominantly urgent instructions inherent in the lower Centers of Consciousness. As you progress to the sixth and seventh levels, you escape from seeing the world through the lower-level filters that bias your perception. In these clear-seeing levels, you are no longer unbalanced by egocentric perspectives. The functioning of the RAS thereby permits a changed flow of energy. It ceases to be an instrument for the gratification or pacification of one's personal conditioning including the mores and folkways of one's "tribe." It begins to function as a vehicle for permitting actions which maintain a continual harmonious flow between your being and your environment at all times. At this level there is a total surrender so that the entire world around you participates in the unfoldment of your life. You are no longer an "individual" in the ordinary sense, but a being voluntarily engaged in the evolvement of consciousness. Such a being encourages the growth of everyone around him by the power of openness, acceptance, and oneness.

As the RAS responds to your efforts to uplevel your programming, you gradually diminish the intricate webs of emotion-backed demands that you mistakenly identified as your "self." You watch your body and mind perform an ever-changing scenario of thoughts, feelings, sensations, and actions. You realize that you have no fixed self or fixed individuality that remains intact. Your name and your ego-based memory no longer give you the illusion of being an "individual." As you grow in consciousness toward the higher levels, you no longer identify the essence of you with your body, your worldly status, your programming, or your rational mind-stuff. You deeply experience your essence as being pure Conscious-awareness that just watches the drama of your life as it is acted out on the myriad stages of the world.

23
THE PROGRAMMING OF HAPPINESS AND UNHAPPINESS

In this chapter we will set forth three types of basic programming for your biocomputer and show the way they operate to produce unhappiness, happiness, or bliss.

DEFINITIONS

First we need three definitions:

1. *Unhappiness* is a psychological state arising from the more or less *continuous* disappointment, frustration, and emotional tension we experience when life repeatedly gives us what we do not want to accept.
2. *Happiness* is a psychological state arising from more or less *continuous* pleasure. Pleasure comes from that which we tell ourselves we want to accept.
3. *Bliss* is a state of *continuous* happiness.

THREE TYPES OF PROGRAMMING

In the Living Love Way to Higher Consciousness, we think in terms of three types of programs for our biocomputer:

1. *Addictive Programming.* This type of programming is tied in with emotional responses produced in the limbic areas of our biocomputer. The use of this type of circuitry makes us experience varying degrees of emotional tension regarding our fears and desires. When our biocomputer processes the incoming sensory information and finds that it threatens the fulfillment of any one of our addictive programs, our consciousness will be dominated by feelings such as fear, anger, resentment, jealousy, or anxiety. Even when we get what we addictively want, *our wanting to keep things that way automatically creates a new addiction!* And we are thereby even more deeply enmeshed in an endless network of emotion-backed demands that yield continuous threat, tension, and unhappiness. Happiness varies inversely with addictions.

2. *Preferential Programming.* When we have Preferential Programming, our biocomputer does not connect the fulfillment or lack of fulfillment with the limbic areas in such a way that emotional responses of fear, anger, jealousy, resentment, etc. are produced. For example, if one has Addictive Programming regarding clear weather during a picnic, he will upset himself if it rains and his "whole day is ruined." If he has Preferential Programming for sunny skies during a picnic, and the rain comes, he just notices that his preference is not being realized. He gathers the things together and continues to enjoy the picnic in the shelter of a gazebo or the car. The flow of the here-and-now appreciation of life is not upset when you have Preferential Programming.

3. *Bliss Programming.* When a person has escaped from all of his Addictive Programs and has enjoyed the happiness-yielding Preferential Programs for a sufficient period of time, it is possible to work toward what we call Bliss Programming. Bliss Programming permits us to achieve *a state of continuous happiness that is not related to any variable life realities.* The nature of all life is that we "win" some and we "lose" some. When we unitively merge with everything, winning and losing are one. Bliss Programming enables us to totally break our dependence on the actions of people or any external conditions (including our bodies).

THE MECHANISM OF UNHAPPINESS

Diagram 1 on the next page shows the mechanism of unhappiness that is associated with the first three Centers of Consciousness—Security, Sensation, and Power. This diagram illustrates the problem of finding happiness when our biocomputer is programmed with fears and desires that are backed up by emotional circuitry. Ninety-nine percent of the people in the world today operate their biocomputers with this type of programming that produces unhappiness in varying degrees. Let's see why.

Let us suppose that you dislike criticism and that your biocomputer is programmed to give you feelings of resentment and anger when someone criticizes you. This may be called "Addictive Dislike Programming" in which you tell yourself, "I dislike criticism." Regardless of our likes or dislikes, the variable life reality is that sometimes we will receive criticism (Condition P—stimulus present) and sometimes we will not receive criticism (Condition N—stimulus not present).

When life gives us Condition P, in which we are criticized, the effect on our consciousness is short-term disappointment, frustration, or suffering. When Condition N occurs and we do not receive criticism, we experience neither disappointment nor pleasure. In other words, it may have no effect on our consciousness. Right now, you are not being criticized, not being beaten up physically, not being starved—and the fact that these things are not happening results in no feeling of either disappointment or pleasure *since your consciousness is not preoccupied with the matter*. However, if one's consciousness is *preoccupied* with a situation, Addictive Dislike Programming, Condition N, will bring pleasure. For example, consider the pleasure a man feels who is pardoned from the electric chair!

Now let's see what happens in those instances in which our biocomputer operates with Addictive Desire Programming. Suppose you have the programming "I desire sex." If the variable life reality offers us Condition P in which sex occurs, the effect on our

Diagram 1 • The Mechanism of Unhappiness

Type of Programming: ADDICTIVE (Emotion-backed) PROGRAMMING
Direction of Energy Flow: Manipulating Subject-Object Relationships
Associated Centers of Consciousness: Security, Sensation, and Power Centers

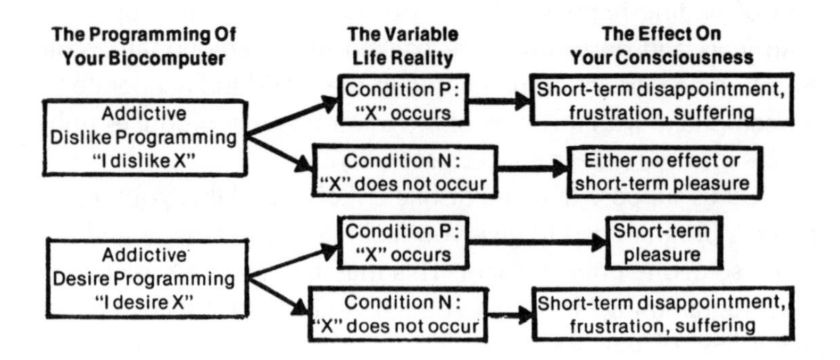

Diagram 2 • The Mechanism of Happiness

Type of Programming: PREFERENTIAL (Non-Emotion-backed) PROGRAMMING
Direction of Energy Flow: Unconditional Acceptance or Love
Associated Centers of Consciousness: Love, Cornucopia, and Conscious-awareness Centers

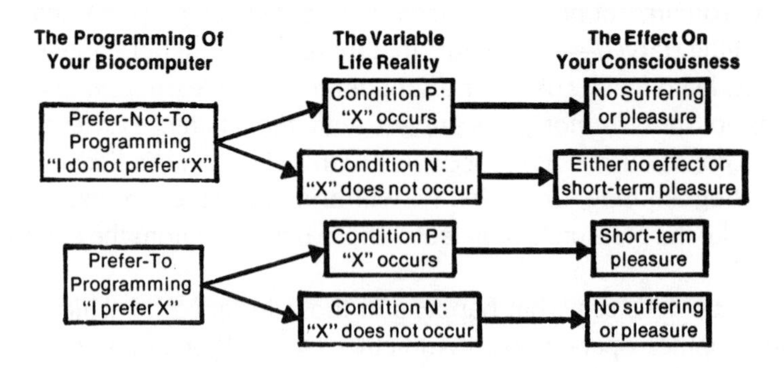

Diagram 3 • The Mechanism of Bliss

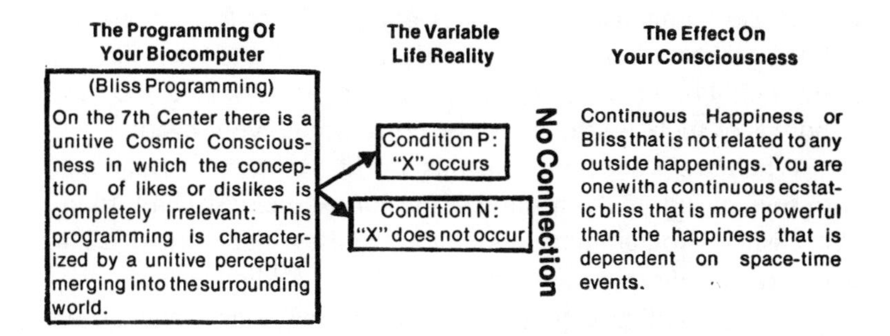

consciousness is to experience a short-term pleasure. However, when we have programmed ourselves to desire sex, and life gives us Condition N in which sex does not occur, we experience short-term disappointment and suffering.

If all of the above four conditions are equally probable, our life will have the following pleasure-suffering ratios:

	Suffering	Pleasure	No Effect
Addictive Dislike Programming, Condition P	25%		
Addictive Dislike Programming, Condition N		12.5%	12.5%
Addictive Desire Programming, Condition P		25.0%	
Addictive Desire Programming, Condition N	25%		
	50%	37.5%	12.5%

The above assumptions imply that half of our life will be spent in experiencing disappointment, frustration, and suffering, 37.5% of the time we will experience pleasure, and 12.5% will be without either suffering or pleasure. This, of course, is a theoretical model of a single addiction to help us understand the mechanism of happiness and unhappiness. Unfortunately, there is a factor that operates to keep us from experiencing pleasure even 37.5% of the time. We can call this factor "The Mosquito Effect."

If you are trying to sleep and there are ten mosquitoes whining around your head at night, you may get up and with considerable effort manage to get rid of most of them. But even though you are 90 per cent effective in eliminating the mosquitoes, it only takes one mosquito whining around your head and biting you to keep you awake. Similarly, *it only takes one dislike or fear or one unfulfilled desire with strong emotional programming to intermittently or even continuously dominate your consciousness.* And you have hundreds of such "mosquitoes" buzzing around your head!

When we were born into this world, we were programmed with several simple desires and fears. For example, we had Addictive Dislike Programming about loud noises that startled us, to which we would respond by crying. We had Addictive Desire Programming regarding eating from time to time. Since infancy, we have expanded the half dozen simple demands we place upon our world into literally hundreds of emotion-backed demands or addictions. Many individuals can use Addictive Desire Programming coupled with Condition N to feel frustration and suffering if they cannot afford the latest model automobile that Detroit is offering as a solution to one's security, sex, and power addictions!

Neurosis and psychosis (as well as the garden variety of anxiety, disappointment, frustration, and suffering) are all directly attributable to the very complex addictive emotional circuitry with which we have burdened ourselves. It is remarkable that human biocomputers function even as well as they do when you consider that every second we are processing millions of incoming nerve impulses to ascertain which patterns have furthering or depriving effects on the myriad of likes and dislikes with which we have blithely programmed ourselves.

Even if life gives us 90 per cent of what we want and protects us from 90 per cent of what we dislike or fear, the remaining 10 per cent will nag our consciousness, dominate our perceptions, perpetuate the churning of our rational mind to "solve the problem," and otherwise keep us from experiencing the state of happiness. For the state of happiness is experienced only when we have an almost continual experience of accepting whatever is here and now in our lives. Just as one mosquito buzzing around our head can keep us awake at night, it may take only one addiction to keep us from experiencing happiness.

THE MECHANISM OF HAPPINESS

A study of Diagram 2 shows that happiness becomes an effective reality in one's life to the degree that we convert our Addictive Programming into Preferential Programming—the kind that does not activate negative emotions. For when we have upleveled our addictions to preferences, we can accept whatever life variables might present themselves without triggering the emotional feelings of disappointment, frustration, and suffering. Suppose, for example, sex is a preference rather than an emotion-backed addiction. When sex does not happen, there is no effect on happiness. But when it does happen, there is a feeling of pleasure.

Similarly, if one has Prefer-not-to Programming such as "I prefer not to have a flat tire on my car," one will not suffer frustration when life throws a flat tire at us (Condition P). We simply observe the reality of the flat tire, and we immediately start doing whatever we need to do to get it changed. When we have Preferential Programming, the flat tire will give us neither pleasure nor suffering. Since our consciousness will be free of the negative feelings triggered by Addictive Programming, we will be free to enjoy whatever there is to enjoy while we're changing the tire. We may notice things in the world around us that would have been otherwise unobserved and thus not enjoyed. Perhaps our consciousness will permit us to appreciate the physical motions we engage in when we efficiently change a tire.

When Condition N occurs coupled with Prefer-not-to Programming, we will experience one of two possible effects depending on whether our consciousness is preoccupied with the matter. If I know air is leaking slowly from a tire and the service station is one block away, I will experience short-term pleasure if the tire takes me to the service station. However, if my consciousness is not at all concerned with the tires, the fact that the tire does not go flat has no effect on my feelings of pleasure or suffering. Hence, Prefer-not-to Programming offers either short-term pleasure or no effect on one's feelings.

Diagram 2 shows that no frustration or suffering is possible in a life situation that has Preferential Programming. Prefer-not-to Programming (Condition P) and Prefer-to Programming (Condition N) do not produce either suffering or pleasure. When we enjoy Preferential Programming, all happenings just pass by as part of our here and now—just like birds flying across the sky. Prefer-to Programming with Condition P brings us pleasure.

If all four conditions are equally probable, two of the four will have no effect on our feelings, one of the four will bring us pleasure, and one will bring either no effect or will bring pleasure.

The Addictive Programming shown in Diagram 1 indicates that the likelihood of suffering exceeds that of pleasure if all four conditions are equally probable. With Preferential Programming, we have vastly improved the pleasure-suffering ratios. Happiness, which is more or less continuous pleasure, is now a real possibility. Based on our simplified theoretical model, here are the improved odds you get *with each addiction you can uplevel to a preference:*

	Suffering	Pleasure	No Effect
Prefer-not-to Programming, Condition P			25.0%
Prefer-not-to Programming, Condition N		12.5%	12.5%
Prefer-to Programming, Condition P		25.0%	
Prefer-to Programming, Condition N			25.0%
	0%	37.5%	62.5%

Since Preferential Programming can insulate us from the "downs" in life, we are then free to enjoy only the "ups." This type of programming is characteristic of the Love Center of Consciousness and the Cornucopia Center of Consciousness. Since a mature adult in these higher consciousness levels will have *many preferential circuits, the opportunities for pleasure are continuous or almost continuous.* For happiness is the continuous or almost continuous experience of getting what you are willing to accept.

When our biocomputers instantly scan the actions and words of all of the people around us in terms of the degree of threat or assistance to realizing our Addictive Programming, *real love is impossible.* Real love, of course, flows from the unconditional acceptance of another person. The love that is most common in our culture is the *illusion of love* in which I can love you only to the extent that you do not threaten my addictions and to the extent that you help me realize my addictive desires. I am trapped in the illusion that I can love you only to the degree that you help me obtain Addictive Desire, Condition P, life situations and help me avoid both Addictive Dislike, Condition P, and Addictive Desire, Condition N, happenings! As soon as you begin to hinder rather than help me with my addictions, this conditional type of love immediately goes out the window!

Real love is possible when I reprogram my biocomputer with Preferential Programming. I can then unconditionally accept everything you do or say—regardless of whether I am willing to do or say the same things myself. For when I have Prefer-to or Prefer-not-to Programming, there is nothing you can do that enables me to make myself feel frustration or suffering. But whenever you happen to play a part in increasing the probability of Condition P when I have Prefer-to Programming, I can regard you as helping me find pleasure in life. In other words, with Preferential Programming, there is no way I can "lose" and there is definitely a way that I can "win." And the "winning" will occur more and more as my consciousness dwells in the Love Center and in the Cornucopia Center.

When you have Preferential Programming in almost all areas of your life, your programming will create a peaceful, loving world for you to live in. The days are past when your Conscious-awareness was dominated by emotion-backed fears or desires. You live in the here and now. You live in a warm Ocean of loving and caring. You have gradually converted your perception of people and things around you from a subject-object basis to a cognitive framework of love and acceptance. By continually living with the programming that yields happiness, contentment, and joy, you open up the possibility for an even further step in consciousness growth.

BLISS PROGRAMMING

The ultimate state in the Living Love Way to Higher Consciousness is generated by "Bliss Programming." The primary characteristic of Bliss Programming is that the feelings of continuous happiness or bliss *are not related to any outside happenings.* In other words, Condition P (in which the desired or preferred thing does occur), or Condition N (in which a desired or preferred thing does not occur) *are irrelevant to one's continuous happiness or bliss.*

When your consciousness is in the Conscious-awareness Center, you witness the drama of your life from a deep, calm place within. On the drama level where your body and mind are agreeing with others, disagreeing with others, earning money, making love, etc., you still have Preferential Programming. But this is all seen as "drama." It is like watching your life on a movie screen. You play your part as an actor in the great cosmic play in which your body and mind and my body and mind (as well as everybody else's) interact on this stage we call the world. But the real you is your Conscious-awareness. So you witness whatever is going on in the drama without fear or desire—without any circuitry that could make you vulnerable to emotional ups and downs. When you go to a movie, you can watch the beautiful happenings or the horrendous happenings—and just enjoy the entire show. *If those things were happening to you, you would be on an up-and-down roller-coaster experience of pleasure and suffering.* But when you see them on a movie screen, they're just so much interesting stuff going by for your perception and enjoyment.

In a similar fashion, when your consciousness is in the Sixth Center, you just witness the drama of your life and that of everyone else. When you are in this Center on a fairly continuous basis, there arises within you a tremendous feeling of well-being and joy. You are filled to brimming with awe and gratitude in the ecstatic knowledge of the inherent goodness of life. Thus the Sixth Center of Consciousness can be regarded as an intermediate stepping stone in which your body and mind may operate as shown in Diagram 1 or 2—but your Conscious-awareness is enjoying the entire show in a manner that is independent of the variable life realities.

The sixth level permits your Conscious-awareness to experience continuous happiness that is not related to anything people do or say or to any of the conditions in the environment around you. Just as the Preferential Programming described in Diagram 2 frees you from the tyranny of the subject-object way of relating to the outside world, the sixth level of consciousness frees you from relating your happiness to any variable life realities. When your consciousness has lived for a period of time in a state of continuous happiness, your ego and rational mind become calmer and quieter. You become deeply attuned to the energies of the people and things around you. Everything is increasingly perceived in an "us" place instead of with "me" vs. "them" perceptions. In this state your consciousness is continually free from subject-object separateness and alienation.

The experience of this greatly expanded consciousness may be preparatory to a transition into the highest Center of Consciousness—the Cosmic Consciousness Center—where all people and things are perceived in a unitive manner. The biocomputer expands its perceptual framework so that every person and every object in the world is felt as if from within. Distinctions between inside and outside (although intellectually clear) are merged in one's experience. All is subject. There is no outside—there is no inside. *There is just "us" happening*—us men, us women, us children, us trees, us automobiles, us rocks, us birds—everything is experienced as a unitive oneness.

It should be clear that this oneness transcends love or unconditional acceptance. There is no longer anybody or anything to accept. Do you unconditionally accept your arm? It just is. It is the ultimate in love. It is not the act of loving someone or something outside of you. Both the outside and inside are one when personal boundaries have disappeared.

THE DIRECTION OF ENERGY FLOW

In the Living Love System we have three cognitive frameworks for perceiving and responding to people and things outside of us:

1. *In a Subject-object Manner* that is characteristic of the Security, Sensation, and Power Centers of Consciousness.

2. *In an Unconditionally Accepting Manner* in which we experience the beauty of unconditional love associated with the Love Center, the Cornucopia Center, and the Conscious-awareness Center.

3. *In a Unitive Perceptual Manner* in which one *feels* no difference between one's self and all of the people and things outside. The capacity for rational discrimination is completely intact. On the rational level one can still perceive people and objects in their aspect of "separateness." But on the feeling level, there is a complete unitive merging into a oneness. This cognitive framework is associated with the Cosmic Consciousness Center.

The direction of energy flow toward the world is associated with *the manner in which we work toward happiness.* On the lower three levels of consciousness, we feel uncritically sure that the way to happiness lies in improving our odds in the middle column entitled "The Variable Life Reality." We put a torrent of energy into subject-object manipulation. We concentrate on preventing that which we addictively dislike, and we try to manipulate and control the people and things in the world to bring about the conditions we addictively desire. But the results are never "enough."

When you realize that no amount of powerful striving is sufficient to bring about happiness through subject-object control of the people and things in the world, you are ready to redirect your energy to the reprogramming of your biocomputer. Your energy flow then helps you become more loving and accepting. You realize that this method of producing happiness is within your conscious ability to achieve. However, it is not necessary to completely withdraw from the drama of manipulating the variable realities in your life. You will even have two of the Twelve Pathways to guide you on the "outside trip."

Two of the Twelve Pathways tell you exactly how to interact with the outside world around you—and the remaining ten Pathways tell you exactly how to work on the inside world *which is yourself.* The Seventh Pathway tells you to openly communicate with everyone so that you no longer feel and think of yourself as separate. The Ninth Pathway says to do anything you want to do *provided* you are tuned in, centered, and loving. Your actions will always be optimal if your head is in the right place. So ACT FREELY—*but don't be addicted to the results.* By following these two Pathways, you will be enormously more effective in changing the people and situations around you than *when you put all your addictive energy into modifying the external conditions of your life.* But this increased power to optimize your environment comes to you **only to the degree that you effectively change yourself using the remaining ten Pathways.**

Some of the conventional methods of consciousness growth may require years or decades for substantial results. The Living Love Methods offer the possibility of rapidly reprogramming your biocomputer so that some of the pleasure and joy of Centers Four and Five may sometimes be experienced in a period of months. It all depends on how much energy you are ready to devote to eliminating frustration and suffering in your life. How intensely do you want to reprogram your biocomputer to produce pleasure and happiness? How soon will you realize that *the only thing you don't have is the direct experience that there's nothing you need that you don't have?*

You should keep your aims realistic and enjoy taking one step at a time. Once a major part of your consciousness resides in the Love Center, you will experience a happiness and beauty in your life that is "enough." Even if you do not progress beyond this Center, you will have a wisdom and effectiveness in your life that will exceed that of most of the people in the world. The consciousness game is the greatest and most genuine of all life games—but one should not get hung up on the spiritual score board. Just enjoy the eternally beautiful here-and-now moment that your life continually offers you. At the end of your journey toward awakening, the only thing you will find is your real self!

24
HOW TO MAKE YOUR LIFE WORK

The main problem in making your life work is that your ego and rational mind keep you trapped in playing out the security, sensation, and power demands that you programmed into your biocomputer during the first few years of your life. You are stuck in these ineffective ruts that make you like a yo-yo bouncing between pain and pleasure. By continually trying to work the unworkable, you blindly repeat your mistakes in a manner that is perhaps more insistent than that of most lower animals.

Werner Erhard has pointed out that even a rat does not usually get hung up in a fruitless repetition of lifetime patterns that are doomed to failure. Let's suppose there are seven tunnels arranged side by side—and you put some cheese at the end of tunnel three. Then you turn a rat loose at the entrances to these tunnels. It will sniff around, maybe look them over, and then in a random fashion explore the tunnels until it finds the one with the cheese. The next time you put the rat near the tunnels, there may be a certain amount of random behavior, but there is a much greater probability that it will go after the cheese in tunnel three. After the rat has done this a few times, it will immediately run down tunnel three to get the cheese.

One day in a rat's life corresponds to about one month in a human life. Suppose that for a period of 60 days the rat finds the cheese at the end of the third tunnel. This would be equivalent to about five years in a human life. Then suppose the cheese is moved from tunnel three to tunnel four. Now we put the rat near the tunnels and he again runs down tunnel three to get the cheese. But the cheese isn't there any longer. The rat will come out, look the scene over, and try tunnel three again. He may repeat this several times. But after a few repeated trials, with no more cheese, the rat will stop going down tunnel three, and start exploring the other ones.

A big difference between a rat and a human being is that a rat won't continue to run down the tunnel that does not provide cheese—whereas a human being may continue to run down the same tunnel for his entire lifetime trying to find the cheese that isn't there! Sooner or later the rat will give up on tunnel three, since it doesn't have a rational mind to continually analyze, compute, and try to prove that the cheese is down tunnel three—because it *used* to be there. A rat cannot go to a library to read books about cheese and how one is supposed to be able to get it. It cannot formulate arguments or make speeches proving that the cheese should really be down tunnel three; and it cannot try to convince fellow rats that there really is cheese down tunnel three even though it is in fact not there. The nervous system of a rat will quickly adapt to the fact that the cheese just isn't where it used to be and it will start looking somewhere else.

When you were two years old, you probably learned that the way to get the cheese (or whatever you wanted) was to scream loudly and try to power-trip your parents. They seemed to control all the cheese. If you cried and fussed enough, by using your Third Center of Consciousness, you could get them to give you candy or let you stay up late at night, or whatever it was that you wanted. You were largely unconscious of the overall picture, and your ego kept your awareness focused on your fears and desires. When you looked at life, it was as though you were looking through the end of a long tunnel and saw only a tiny spot of the world at the end of the tunnel. The overall picture of life was blocked out by the sides of the tunnel. Your immature biocomputer permitted your fears and desires to project on the screen of your consciousness only a tiny slice of the life realities around you. You had no real choice in your life, because you had no wide-range perception of the people and events around you.

By age two, you had deeply programmed yourself by using crying to force changes in the people and things around you. At that time in your life, this was one of the few ways you had to get what you wanted from the world. It is difficult to explain to a two-year old that the lower three levels of consciousness generate unhappiness, and that the really big stash of cheese is located at the end of the Love Tunnel and the Cornucopia Tunnel. How do you tell a young child that there is only a little dab of low-grade cheese *which will never be enough* at the end of the Security Tunnel, Sensation Tunnel, and Power Tunnel? How do you show a young child that he can have all the cheese that he could ever want by harmonizing his energies with the flow of the people and situations around him? How do you explain to a crying child that loving acceptance of the here and now is the only way that brings continuous happiness in life?

And so you get used to running down the Security Tunnel, Sensation Tunnel, and Power Tunnel hunting for the cheese. The fact that you are reading these words right now indicates that you are getting suspicious about the first three tunnels, and are beginning to explore the Love Tunnel and the Cornucopia Tunnel. You know there must be more cheese in life than you have been getting. Diagram 1 shows you why your life hasn't been working, and Diagram 2 shows you how to clearly start getting the cheese that has always been waiting for you in life but which you couldn't get because you persisted in trying to find it down the wrong tunnel. Your life is naturally good. It has always been workable. It's just that your biocomputer kept making the same *perceptual mistakes* over and over and over again.

Why isn't your life working as it should? What is pouring sand in the gears? The problem is simple: your programming continually directs you to find happiness *by trying to change the life energies around you.* You put most of your attention and energy into trying to manipulate the people and situations in your life. Since you found some cheese at the end of tunnel three during the immature, early years of your life, your ego and your rational mind continue to direct most of your energy into changing the life energies around you to fit your addictive inner programming (see the top box in Diagram 1 on next page.)

Now let's follow the cycle around to discover how you create a "hell" from the world in which you live—when heaven is there all the time! The words and actions of people are sent by your various senses into the analytical and interpretive sections of your biocomputer. When outside patterns do not fit your inner programmed patterns, you respond with negative emotional feelings such as anger, fear, jealousy, resentment, etc., and create your experience of unhappiness (see right-hand box and bottom box in Diagram 1).

This leads you to the fourth phase of the Wheel of Unhappiness. You then begin to criticize and reject yourself and others. You communicate with words, vocal tones, facial expressions, and body gestures that either you are rotten or the world is rotten, or perhaps both. Your rational mind criticizes other people and finds fault with them. It gives you reasons why they are "fools," "idiots," "uncaring monsters," "evil beings," or whatever. Or you may use programming that turns your rational mind against yourself and creates the experience that you are inadequate, hopeless, inept, dumb, inferior, crazy, or whatever.

This alienating subject-object feedback *then begins to change the behavior of people and the characteristics of the life conditions around you* (we're back to the top box in Diagram 1). In other words, your negative feedback begins to make a dramatic change in the response of the people and conditions around you. You thus create an environment of antagonistic people and situations. Now the Wheel of Unhappiness begins to turn and the people around you begin to respond with words and actions that reflect their negative feelings to your criticism and rejection. Then this feeds back into your emotional programming and triggers more anger, fear, jealousy, or up-tight emotions. And you react by criticizing yourself more and criticizing others more. (See left-hand box in Diagram 1.) This feeds back into the people and situations around you and turns them against you even more. . . . And things become even worse in your life as the cycle turns and turns and turns in a downward

DIAGRAM 1
How You Create Unhappiness In Your Life

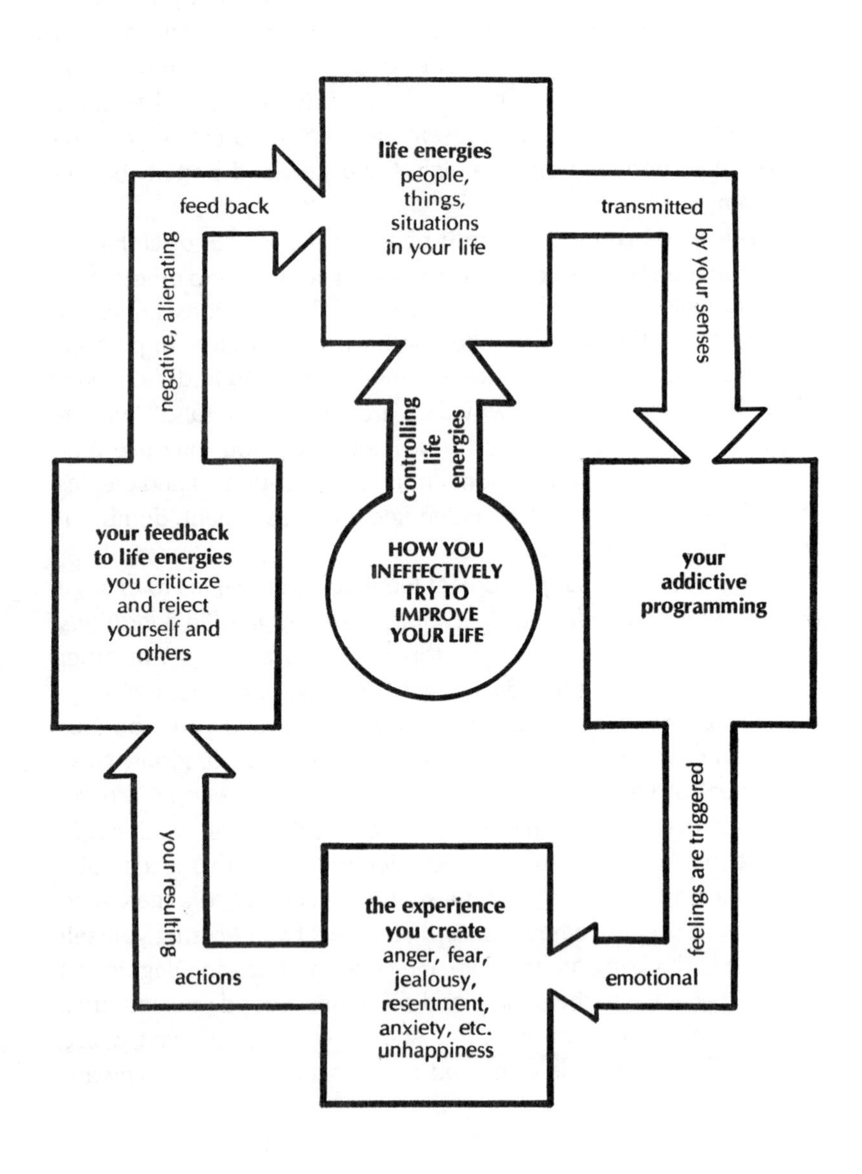

DIAGRAM 2
How You Create Happiness In Your Life

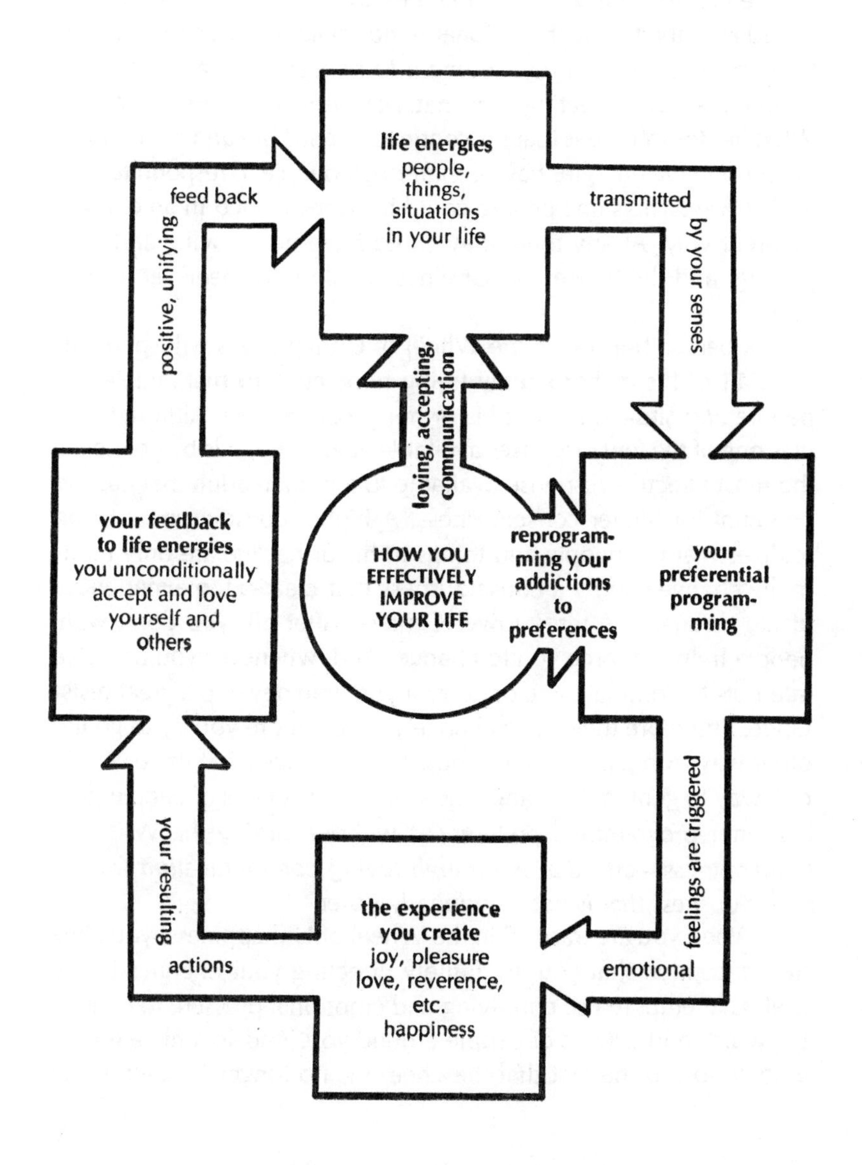

spiral. Your rational mind may accept this downward spiral as proof that your life is impossible, that people are horrible, and that there is no way of "making it" in life.

A human being trapped in the Wheel of Unhappiness does not realize that the world is not "doing it" to him. The defenses of ego (aided and abetted by the rational mind) make it extremely difficult for him to realize *that he is doing it to himself.* He can prove that people are really treating him that way. And they are, of course. What he doesn't see is that *his continuous criticism and rejection of the outside life energies have conditioned people to respond to him in that way.* The same people could have responded in an entirely different way. At any time, they could have been loving and supporting, and the Wheel of Happiness could have been set in motion.

A person trapped in the Wheel of Unhappiness will spend almost all of his or her energy trying hopelessly to manipulate the people and situations to fit his or her programming. Although this was one of the few responses available at age two, it is by no means the most effective response available to a human adult that has the potential for higher consciousness. A higher consciousness being realizes that the people and things in his or her life are only minimally changeable by a consciousness that creates the experiences of life through the three lower Centers. After all, you don't want people trying to force you to change. And, whenever you perceive attempts to dominate you or control you, you develop a great resistance. The more they try to change you, the more you try to go the other way. A higher consciousness being realizes that there is only one way to genuinely change the words and actions of people to fit his inner programmed preferences without turning the Wheel of Unhappiness—*and that is through loving communication from a consciousness that is not emotionally upset.*

When you are trapped in the Wheel of Unhappiness, you have no conception that you are futilely directing your energies in the useless attempt to use conniving and emotional pressure to change the words and actions of people around you. And so, unlike the rat who adapts to the fact that the cheese is no longer located in the third tunnel, you keep yourself trapped by trying to manipulate and change the people and things in your life. *The problems you had at age two are gone—yet you are unconsciously playing out the methods you used back then.* **These obsolete solutions deprive you of the opportunity to fully experience and enjoy your life.**

When you apply a heavy enough power trip, you may make certain changes in the life energies around you. But if you were conscious of the enormous separation and alienation that your criticism and manipulation creates with the people around you, you would realize that you cannot afford the price in lost happiness that you pay for the precious few changes you may force on the surface. The only changes that you can make, without paying a large penalty, are those changes that gently and easily happen when you make a loving communication. When that won't do it, you should work on releasing yourself from your inner addictions and emotion-backed demands that are controlling or dominating your consciousness.

How do you stop the downward spiraling of the Wheel of Unhappiness and start converting it into an upward Spiral of Happiness? You need to redirect your energy from trying to change the outer life energies, to changing your inner programming (see right-hand box in Diagram 2). There are no methods available *that will enable you to successfully change all of the outer life energies around you to fit your inner emotional programming.* You could have the power of a king, the prestige of a movie star, or the knowledge of a Ph.D., but the condition of your life would still remain the same—*you win some and you lose some.* By using the Five Methods of Living Love, you have the capacity to change your own inner programming. There is a huge supply of cheese waiting for you, but you can only get to it by working on your own inner programming so that, here and now, you can emotionally accept the people and situations in your life.

When you work on your inner adaptation, by reprogramming the emotion-backed demands you place on people and situations in your life, you will find that the life situations and energies that used to create unhappiness will be neutral or positive in their effect on your happiness. Your energy, perceptiveness, and ability to love unconditionally will make you invulnerable to suffering. And so the third phase of Diagram 2 shows that you begin to feed back a loving acceptance of the people and situations around you.

Just as your criticism strongly affects the life energies around you, your positive feedback can begin to powerfully affect the life energies around you. The more you lovingly accept people in your life, without conditions, the more you free them to enjoy being around you. Their egos and rational minds do not have to stay in a paranoid or defensive place, and *when they are with you they can begin to experience themselves free of security, sensation, and power addictions that you formerly reflected or set off in them.* This frees their energy to experience themselves and you without a "tunnel vision" effect. They begin to feel free and liberated around you. They develop a deep trust that you will remain tuned-in, centered, and loving no matter what they do. They can just relax and enjoy, and begin to groove in a loving, mutually supportive space with you.

Instead of negatively affecting the life energies around you, so as to put people even more out of phase with your programming (as in Diagram 1), people may now begin to change their feelings in ways that begin to fit your Preferential Programming. And if they don't change, it doesn't matter—because it was only a "preference" anyway. Since you are largely free from Addictive Programming, they don't have to walk around like they're tip-toeing on eggs all the time. They can just relax and flow with their own inner vibrations and energies for they know that you won't make yourself upset, regardless of what they may do or say. As they begin to love you in a deeper and deeper way, their egos may begin directing their energy to do the things that you prefer. And this can stimulate joyous feelings that create the experience of increasing happiness in your life.

Your upleveling of addictions to preferences enables you to love more and more (see Third Phase of Diagram 2), and the Wheel of Happiness begins to turn. For your love modifies the life energies of people and frees them to love you and serve you, which feeds back into your Preferential Programming so that even more enjoyment and happiness are created. Then your feelings of love multiply. Since your loving feedback to the life energies around you is further intensified, the Wheel of Happiness turns and turns and turns in an upward spiral—thus creating loving, peaceful feelings that spring from a deep harmony with the here and now of your life.

Just as you created the experience of unhappiness in your life by your continual negative feedback into the life energies around you, you have now, in a god-like manner, created the experience of happiness in your life. You have created a "miracle"—you are no longer an "effect" of the world around you—you have become a "cause"—a creative source. Your higher consciousness has created the beautiful world you live in.

Now you know why your life is naturally good, how your life really wants to work, and how your programming has been the only roadblock to your experiencing continuous happiness in life. You know that you have the capacity to create the experience of happiness or the experience of unhappiness in your life. **It all depends on the quality and quantity of critical, rejecting energy or accepting, loving energy that you feed back into the people and situations around you.** You see clearly how you have kept your life from working.

You can now begin to demonstrate the miracle of creating happiness in your life. And by doing this, you are doing the most you can for other people—for the most effective way to help them is to become a happy, loving, conscious being. Lectures or exhortations are only a sham that can be spotted as another subtle method of manipulation and control—unless you are actually off the Wheel of Unhappiness, and have the Wheel of Happiness turning joyously in your life. And once you realize that "happiness runs in a circular motion," you won't need to lecture or exhort other people to convince them. They will be picking up on how you have jumped from the Wheel of Unhappiness to the Wheel of Happiness, and they will be asking you how you did it. And then you can share with them the Methods of the Living Love Way so that they can begin to create the experience of continuous happiness in their lives.

25
THE PURPOSE OF YOUR LIFE

A first step in your growth toward higher consciousness is to see clearly the enormous expenditure of fruitless energy that you are now putting into living out your addictive programming. *Every* addiction you have programmed into your head will separate you and make you suffer to a greater or lesser degree. Your feelings of disappointment, irritability, anger, jealousy, or fear are giving you urgent messages: "Here is an addiction that you must reprogram into a preference in order to live an effective and joyous life."

The remarkable thing about growing into higher consciousness is that it is only *the release from the emotion-backed inner addiction* that is required—you do not necessarily need to *change your actions.* If you are addicted to over-eating chocolate cream puffs, the problem lies not in the action of putting chocolate cream puffs into your mouth—the problem lies *wholly in the circuitry of your biocomputer* that makes you a slave to this inner desire. When you use the Five Living Love Methods for reprogramming your addictions, the outer behavior will take care of itself. You may from time to time eat chocolate cream puffs, but you are freed from an inner addiction that dominates your consciousness. You will not keep a fresh supply in the house. You will no longer let a large part of your calories be wasted on such relatively "empty" food with unfortunate consequences to your health. When you uplevel this addiction to a preference, you may still enjoy a cream puff from time to time—*but you can also enjoy life if you do not eat cream puffs.* And so the energy that was previously drained into an addiction can now flow into channels that add to your happiness and joy.

When you reprogram an addiction, you may find that you have no further interest in the external actions that you had been engaging in. Or when you reprogram an addiction and uplevel it to a preference, you may find that there will be no change in your external actions. For example, if you uplevel an addiction for not washing dishes to a preference, you may find that you are now able to consciously wash dishes. Your addictive programming will no longer operate to make you unhappy when you are doing this necessary job.

The Living Love Way to Higher Consciousness does not teach you to *repress* the emotional programming that separates you from other people (for this causes psychosomatic diseases) or to *express* this duality and alienation (which is the traditional method of psychology and psychiatry). To go into higher consciousness, you must eliminate the *cause* of all feelings of duality, isolation, and separation that keep you from loving yourself and everyone and everything around you. The Twelve Pathways, the Seven Centers of Consciousness, and the Five Methods enable you *to eliminate the cause of your unhappiness.*

You begin to realize that a direct and rapid way to find happiness is available through using your negative emotional feelings to show you which parts of your biocomputer need reprogramming in order to enjoy every moment of your life. In the past, you have used the majority of your energy trying to control, dominate, and change the people and situations in your life. Now this energy can be channeled into the Five Methods to get free of the addictions that keep one trapped in greed, anger, and delusion.

And then a most remarkable thing happens. When you reprogram your addictions, you will find that you can love everyone unconditionally—including yourself. As long as people were *objects to be manipulated* to help you achieve your addictions, real love (unconditional acceptance of another person) was impossible. You now find that you can love in a profoundly beautiful way that you never knew existed before.

This new dimension of love produces a miracle in your life. For it now makes you open to new experiences, new people, and new activities. When you begin to live in the fourth level of consciousness, you no longer experience any person or any situation as a threat. You find that you now have everything you need to be happy.

You will continually marvel at the way that the people and situations in your life are harmoniously functioning to meet your real needs. And your consciousness may go back to the day when you first discovered the Living Love book that helped to show you the way to bring about this miracle in your life. But did *you* discover it? Wasn't it the people and conditions of your life that offered it to you—because of your openness? Trace the major things that have happened to you since the day you first began your conscious growth toward becoming a more receptive, effective, and wiser being. You will find that you have interacted with the people and conditions of your life to help you make wiser and wiser choices that have accelerated your continuing growth into higher consciousness. We're all on the journey together!

It feels so unbelievably great to be liberated from the consciousness-dominating barrage of desires, demands, expectations, inflexible patterns, models of how the world should treat you—addictions of every kind. Anyone watching you might see you doing more or less the same things you used to do, but there is a *new you* doing them. You still go to the grocery store to buy food, but you do it with a biocomputer that now permits you to enjoy every minute of the experience. No matter how many items you can't find, or no matter how long you have to wait in line, you can no longer make yourself feel frustrated, disappointed, or create suffering of any sort.

Your trip to a grocery store becomes a beautiful experience. And your smiles, your helpfulness, and your vibrations of love affect those around you. Your new non-addictive being changes the path of your daily doings from a tiresome drudgery into an energy-producing delightful panorama that passes before your eyes. You find that you have discovered that all of the people in the grocery store are awakening beings who are there to help you in your journey toward higher consciousness. And you have the deep satisfaction of knowing that by living a higher consciousness life, you are also doing the most (without any striving) to help other beings in their growth toward higher consciousness.

A beautiful thing about higher consciousness is that what is best for you is best for everyone else. When you begin to live on the Fourth or higher Levels, your radiant inner being creatively changes the feelings and actions of the people and the vibrations of the situations that you come in contact with. You give them the greatest gift of all—you tune in to them at the beautiful place that is behind their lower-consciousness games. You flow harmoniously with them at the place on the fourth level where they are pure love. And this can even be done with nothing more than a loving eye-to-eye contact or smile. By relating to that place in them where they are love, you temporarily put their consciousness into a higher place. This *way of being,* more than anything you could ever achieve externally in life, becomes the source of that feeling of conscious satisfaction about the "rightness" and the meaningfulness of your life.

A wonderful thing about the Living Love Way is that you can do it "alone" if need be. You can regard others as actors on the cosmic stage who are here to make you aware of your addictions. They are helping you by creating situations in which your emotions reveal the hiding places of your addictions. Regardless of whether they know of the inner work that you are doing, everything they do or say helps you grow into higher consciousness. Even though they may be driven by addictive programming that makes them irritated or hostile, *you can use all of their actions, emotional expressions, and words to help you become free of your addictions.* And as you reprogram your biocomputer and liberate yourself, they will begin to notice the extraordinary joy, freedom, and love that radiates from you irrespective of what they do or say. This transformation will be so unexpected and amazing to them that they will want to know what is happening inside of you. And when they ask, you can then joyously share the keys that you discovered for unlocking happiness.

You can show them how it is all found inside—independent of the changing world of people, objects, and situations. And if they are ready to hear, they will be amazed at the simplicity of the method for growing into higher consciousness. It simply means upleveling all their addictions into preferences. It will take them a while to *really understand the awesome vastness of their addictions*. But the results in increased happiness and ability to love will arrive so rapidly that they will know they have at last found the answer to making life work. And by helping themselves, they have now helped you grow even more rapidly toward the higher levels of consciousness. You will have been given the opportunity to explain it, and you will have discovered additional insights you need for your growth. Their vibrations of growing love and expanded consciousness are helping you live in a more beautiful world. They help you liberate even more energy for your own journey.

As you learn to process all of your incoming sensory data and your thoughts from the higher Centers of Consciousness, the "problems" in your life disappear. As a result of living in the Love Center and learning to harmonize your energies with the energies of the people in the world around you, you are permitting the world to give you the optimal that is obtainable for you. This tunes you in to experience deeply the marvelous way in which your life is naturally rich and abundant. Your growing freedom from addictions permits you to increasingly love everyone unconditionally—including yourself. And your love kindles the love of other people. The energy of mutual helpfulness flows in loving relationships in a way that you previously obstructed by the subject-object way you treated the people around you.

Your constantly increasing flow of energy enables you to deeply feel that the world will automatically provide you with more than you need to be happy. You do not have to fight, cajole, force, cleverly scheme, or dominate your consciousness with comparisons of what is, what was, or what should be in the future. You may say, "What's the worst that could happen?" And then you may say, "Well, that would be all right—I can still live and be happy even if that happens." And you find that life usually has a miraculous way of giving you an optimal amount of whatever it is that you need to be happy, fulfilled, and joyous.

Here's some good news. It is not necessary to be one hundred per cent free of emotion-backed addictions in order to experience continuous happiness. However, you must be *almost* free of addictions in order to keep them from exerting a downward drag that produces the experience of unhappiness. Happiness is a general level of good feeling that you generate when life gives you what you are prepared to accept. This general level is not affected *if you can quickly recover* from any experience of fear, anger, resentment, irritation, etc. The state of unhappiness develops when an addictive experience goes on and on. This state becomes intense when you let one addiction after another pile up on top of you so that you are loading your biocomputer with several addictive models and expectations to which the world is not conforming. *If, within several minutes or even an hour or so, you can get on top of an addiction, it will not usually affect your happiness level.* If you trigger anger, for example, you can actually enjoy being angry for a short while. However, if you continuously make yourself angry, unhappiness inevitably develops because of the continued hyperactivity of your autonomic nervous system, the adverse feedback of the surrounding world, and the overwhelming cumulative effect of subject-object relationships—with resulting lowered energy, lowered insight, and lowered love. If you are now using the Living Love Methods to free yourself from addictive programming, you deeply know that your emotional feelings of separateness are simply vestiges of your previous lower consciousness programming. You will then quickly rid yourself of any current nonsense whenever you catch yourself triggering fear, anger, or irritation.

Thus perfection in eliminating all of your addictive patterns is not necessary in order for you to be happy all of the time. For example, to be an effective typist one does not have to be perfect, *but one must be a conscious typist and be able to recognize and correct errors quickly and almost automatically.* For most practical purposes, a page that has been consciously corrected on the spot is just as good as a page that was typed perfectly to begin with.

Wher you have achieved a high degree of proficiency at using the Living Love Way—when you see your life as a drama in which you use everyone and everything as a teaching that helps you to become more conscious—you will find that you will get to the point where small bits of your old addictive programming are just an occasional nuisance to you. When you live in the Fourth and Fifth Centers of Consciousness most of the time, an infrequent *quick dip* into the first three Centers is of little significance to you. Therefore, you don't have to be addicted to perfection—just get on with your inner work. It will all happen at the rate that is just right for you.

When a person becomes an expert at emotionally accepting the here and now in life (and uplevels all addictions to preferences), does he lose his effectiveness in doing his part to combat social injustices such as war, prejudice, economic exploitation, environmental pollution, etc.? If one emotionally accepts everything, would he want to change anything? When one's experience of the here and now is no longer generated from an urgent security or power consciousness, does the Love or Cornucopia consciousness enable a person to be a socially responsible member of society? Are anger, frustration, and hatred needed to build a better world? Will love consciousness release the energy needed to create a paradise on earth?

As long as a person operates from the lower three Centers of Consciousness, he perpetuates the *cause* of all social injustice—the treating of people as though they were "others," the subject-object attitude toward people, the determination to get what one wants without finding the "us" place, and the inability to love people unconditionally. The person who lives in the Fourth Center *may make an even deeper contribution to correcting the disharmony of the world than the individual who works from the lower three Centers.* By one's being and actions, one is correcting the cause of social injustice—instead of just treating the symptoms. Even though a person at the Fourth Center may carry a placard, write letters, attend meetings, and do other things designed to encourage people to find the "us" space, he will do it from a love consciousness that may often be more effective in reaching the people that he wishes to change. A Living Lover is free to exert energy in either fighting the symptoms of disharmony in the world or to expend energy in correcting the cause of man's inhumanity to man—*which cause is always the addictions connected with the perception of life from the lower three centers.*

A Living Lover continually experiences the beauty and perfection of the world. He understands that we create events in order to give us the experience we need to get free from the lower Centers. A Living Lover constantly experiences a harmony and love above and beyond the daily drama of addictive strife, and at the same time he experiences the beauty and perfection of expending his energy to uplevel the security, sensation, and power consciousness of one's fellow beings into the Love Center of Consciousness.

It's all perfect now, and it's also perfect to expend energy to effect changes! To the degree that the world reflects the actions of individuals experiencing life through security, sensation, and power consciousness, the beauty and perfection of the world will consist of *its ability to teach us what we need to know to uplevel our consciousness to the Fourth Center—both individually and collectively.* To the extent that the world is populated by individuals who generate their experience from the Fourth or higher Centers of Consciousness, the beauty and perfection are reflected by the continuous enjoyment of the Cornucopia that life is giving to us.

As you get on with your inner work on yourself, you develop a deep gut-level confidence that the Cornucopia will happen *automatically* to the degree that you are free from processing your thoughts through an addictive security, sensation, and power consciousness. You realize you don't have to worry any more about enough loving friends, enough food and shelter, enough enjoyable things to do, enough sex, avoiding catastrophes that would ruin your life, keeping people from pushing you around, etc. Based on your experience, you gradually develop the feeling that when you use the Twelve Pathways as your guide in everyday life situations, you can totally rely on the flowing harmony of the interactions of your energy and the energies outside of you to continuously give you more than you need to be happy. You realize that you can just live your life in a gentle non-striving, flowing way. You realize that life is really set up to enable us to live happy, peaceful, fulfilling lives—and that it is only the automated dance of our security, sensation, and power addictions that keeps us from experiencing that we have more than we need to be happy.

By getting rid of our emotion-backed addictions, demands, and expectations that make us reject what is, we discover that we can at all times enjoy the many "strawberries" that life is offering us instead of dominating our consciousness with the "tigers." As we learn to totally surrender to what is, we at last find more security, more delightful sensations, more powerful effectiveness, and more love than we could ever need to be happy. Then the Cornucopia of life unfolds in the most marvelous way—and we live continuously in a warm, friendly, loving universe that we have created by our higher consciousness.*

And so, hand in hand, we journey down the river of our lives toward the vast Ocean of Oneness that is our source and our destiny. At last we have the profound joy of knowing:

*** In the audiotape *Handbook to Higher Consciousness*, you can hear Ken personally present many of the principles in this book. See page 217 for more information.**

The
purpose
of our lives
is to be free of
all addictive traps,
and thus

become One

with the Ocean of
Living Love.

APPENDIX 1
THE LIVING LOVE THEORY OF HAPPINESS

1. *The Problem.* Most people are trapped in patterns of consciousness that result in widespread unhappiness, alienation, fears, continuous conflict, etc. Instead of realizing the "cornucopia" that life offers us, our programming creates lives characterized by tension and a low level of enjoying life. The way we currently process, interpret, perceive, and act upon incoming stimuli is responsible for our inability to be happy one hundred per cent of the time. We are all beautiful beings but our lower consciousness security, sensation, and power programming causes us to make ourselves unhappy.

2. *Basic Principle. Happiness varies inversely with one's addictions.* Addictions are programmed expectations, demands, "absolute necessities," desires, or models of how the world should be that automatically trigger negative emotions such as anger, fear, jealousy, anxiety, irritation, resentment, grief, etc. Every addiction makes one vulnerable to suffering. When one understands how the experience of happiness and unhappiness is generated, it becomes evident that all unhappiness is due to addictive models that determine our perception and motivation. Even physical pain does not produce unhappiness unless one has an addiction for being free from pain. It is the addiction, not the pain, that generates suffering.

3. *The Predicament of Life.* The changing energy stream of life in which we live satisfies some addictions and leaves others unsatisfied. In other words, we win some and we lose some. Even when we win, we then unwittingly create another addictive de-

mand that must be lived out in a robot-like fashion. We usually attempt to change our win-lose odds by more money, knowledge, prestige, or power. These lines of endeavor never make *enough* change in the "win-some, lose-some" pattern to produce a high level enjoyment of life. Our expectations and demands continue to dominate our consciousness and create an unsatisfactory experience of life as long as we have any addictive programming.

4. *A Dilemma.* Unsatisfied addictions dominate our consciousness, make us unable to love unconditionally, keep our rational minds churning, lead our consciousness into "futuring and pasting" instead of enjoying the here and now, and make us trigger negative emotions in an attempt to manipulate the people in the world around us. The unfulfilled addictive demands produce the experience of suffering and unhappiness. The addictions we satisfy give us only brief pleasure. That which satisfies an addiction soon tends to form a new addiction that our nervous system indiscriminately protects and enhances. Regardless of whether or not we get what we want, we are still vulnerable to fear, grief, or anger that can generate the experience of unhappiness.

5. *The Unworkable Solution.* Our ancestors, throughout eons of jungle life, developed nervous systems that effectively guarded our species against external dangers. Over 99% of the people in the world today are stuck with nervous systems that usually operate by blaming the outside world for any problems they experience. We organize our perceptions and energies into trying to make our lives work by programming that is ultra efficient at comparing the outside world with our inner addictive models—*thus triggering emergency alarms of anger, fear, grief, frustration, or jealousy when they do not correspond.* When we operate on lower consciousness levels, we trigger emotions that generate forceful actions in an attempt to change the outside world so that it corresponds with our security, sensation, and power addictions. The result is a roller-coasting between pleasure and pain (which we try to ameliorate by increasing our skill at manipulation) meanwhile maintaining a social veneer of politeness, diplomacy, and a shallow degree of warmth and love. Conscious people always have a choice of

whether to try to modify the actions of people around them *or to change their responses to the incoming stimuli.*

6. *The Way To Happiness.* The practical solution to the problem of continuously enjoying our lives is to re-train our biocomputers so that the first response to a life situation is to harmonize our energies with the outside world instead of trying to force the outside world to fit our inner patterns. Unconditionally loving communication (which is not addicted to results) will usually permit the adjustments to occur that we need for harmonizing our energies. Every addiction leaves us vulnerable; preferences enable us to continually enjoy life. When our biocomputers operate from preferential programming, our happiness is not affected—regardless of whether the outside world fits our preferences or not. This permits us to enjoy the here and now of our lives, to remain centered at all times, to love unconditionally, to avoid subject-object manipulation, to feel secure and invulnerable, to increase our insight and perceptiveness, and to feel at home in the world.

When our biocomputers are retrained to interact with our world in these ways, we find that life gives us the optimum in security, sensations, power, and love. The Living Love Way does far more than enable a person to passively adjust to the here and now of his or her life; it is a dynamic system for retraining one's consciousness to live an effective life that is continuously enjoyable.

Appendix 2
Summary—The Five Parts of Living Love

THE LAW OF HIGHER CONSCIOUSNESS:	**Love Everyone Unconditionally—Including Yourself.**

THE FIVE METHODS PLUS THE INSTANT CONSCIOUSNESS DOUBLER:

1. *Memorize* the Twelve Pathways and apply them to your problems.
2. *Be aware* at all times of which Center of Consciousness you are using to perceive your world.
3. *Become* more consciously conscious of the cause-effect relationship between your addictions and the resulting unhappiness.
4. *Use the Catalyst* ALL WAYS US LIVING LOVE as a tool for cognitive centering.
5. *Use the Consciousness Focusing Method* to accelerate the reprogramming of heavy addictions.

plus the

Instant Consciousness Doubler:

Expand your love, your consciousness, and your loving compassion by experiencing everything that everyone does or says as though you had done or said it.

THE TWELVE PATHWAYS:

Freeing Myself

1. *I am freeing myself* from security, sensation, and power addictions that make me try to forcefully control situations in my life, and thus destroy my serenity and keep me from loving myself and others.

2. *I am discovering* how my consciousness-dominating addictions create my illusory version of the changing world of people and situations around me.

3. *I welcome the opportunity* (even if painful) that my minute-to-minute experience offers me to become aware of the addictions I must reprogram to be liberated from my robot-like emotional patterns.

Being Here Now

4. *I always remember* that I have everything I need to enjoy my here and now—unless I am letting my consciousness be dominated by demands and expectations based on the dead past or the imagined future.

5. *I take full responsibility* here and now for everything I experience, for it is my own programming that creates my actions and also influences the reactions of people around me.

6. *I accept myself completely* here and now and consciously experience everything I feel, think, say, and do (including my emotion-backed addictions) as a necessary part of my growth into higher consciousness.

Interacting With Others

7. *I open myself genuinely* to all people by being willing to tully communicate my deepest feelings, since hiding in any degree keeps me stuck in my illusion of separateness from other people.

8. *I feel with loving compassion* the problems of others without getting caught up emotionally in their predicaments that are offering them messages they need for their growth.

9. *I act freely* when I am tuned in, centered, and loving, but if possible I avoid acting when I am emotionally upset and depriving myself of the wisdom that flows from love and expanded consciousness.

Discovering My Conscious-awareness

10. *I am continually calming* the restless scanning of my rational mind in order to perceive the finer energies that enable me to unitively merge with everything around me.

11. *I am constantly aware* of which of the Seven Centers of Consciousness I am using, and I feel my energy, perceptiveness, love, and inner peace growing as I open all of the Centers of Consciousness.

12. *I am perceiving everyone,* including myself, as an awakening being who is here to claim his or her birthright to the higher consciousness planes of unconditional love and oneness.

THE SCALE FOR KNOWING YOUR CENTER OF CONSCIOUSNESS AT EACH MOMENT:

The Seven Centers of Consciousness:

1. The Security Center
2. The Sensation Center
3. The Power Center
4. The Love Center
5. The Cornucopia Center
6. The Conscious-awareness Center
7. The Cosmic Consciousness Center

THE PURPOSE OF OUR LIVES:

The purpose of our lives is to be free of all addictive traps, and thus become One with the Ocean of Living Love.

Appendix 3
How to Accelerate Your Growth in the Living Love Way

Here are eight ways in which you can enormously accelerate your growth toward higher consciousness:

1. *Reread This Book.* On your first reading you will begin to develop an intellectual understanding. This is only a first step toward illuminating your life with the Living Love Way. To bring the words and ideas of the book into your moment-to-moment consciousness, repeated readings are absolutely necessary. If you wish to grow at the fastest rate, read at least five pages of this book every night just before going to sleep. If you do this constantly, you will be giving yourself a maximum opportunity to liberate the hidden splendor within you.

2. *Underline Freely.* Underline every sentence in the book that is especially significant to you. These will be the parts that you are now ready to receive in your here and now stream of consciousness. This prepares you for your next step in opening toward a deeper acceptance and application of the Living Love Way in your daily life. And gradually more and more of the book will be underlined as a sign of your growing integration.

3. *Give Yourself the Benefit of All Five Methods.* Let all of the Five Methods help you in your growth. If you find that you are not

using one of the Methods, concentrate on that Method during the next month. To avoid imbalance and lopsidedness, you should use all of the Five Methods.

4. *Avoid a Spiritual Soup.* When you find your spiritual path, put your full energy into perfecting your practice of the methods associated with your chosen path. If you constantly shop around, compare, and experiment with different combinations from various spiritual paths, you may fail to get the benefit in depth that would be found by intensely devoting yourself to a single path.

5. *Surrender.* Your spiritual growth will be directly correlated with the degree to which you surrender to the methods of your chosen path. And just what are you really surrendering? You are only surrendering the low-level programming that now keeps you disappointed, upset, and unhappy in varying degrees.

6. *Intensity of Desire for Growth.* Your complete inner dedication to your growth into higher consciousness is the single most important determinant of your spiritual development. Without an intense inner commitment, you are just a dilletante playing spiritual games. When spiritual growth is the most important thing in your life, the full miracle of love and oneness will unfold in your life.

7. *Offer the Living Love Way to Others.* Remember that your life works better when you are surrounded by loving, fulfilled, happy beings. You will grow when you offer the system to others—but always wait until they clearly indicate an openness to receive your gift of explaining how consciousness growth works. You must be very perceptive in offering the Living Love Way to other people *so that you do not create a duality when you are striving for oneness.* Do not try to "sell" it to them or make them feel that this is the only answer to happiness in their life. This would probably trigger their resistance programming. Instead, offer it by sharing your experience in applying the Five Methods. Set aside all pride and let them see *your inner struggle to work on yourself*—but don't insist that they should work on themselves in a similar way. Perhaps, without any words of recommendation, you might simply leave a copy of the *Handbook* on the desk of a close friend. As a

part of your consciousness growth, learn to love everyone unconditionally regardless of whether he or she is interested in what you are doing.

8. *Attend a Consciousness Growth Training.* By participating in a workshop, you will have the opportunity to work with other people using the Living Love Methods. Weekend, one week, and longer trainings are given regularly at the Ken Keyes College in Coos Bay, Oregon and in major cities throughout the United States.

For information on trainings, other books by Ken, cassettes of some of his workshop talks, and the location of local study groups in your area, write to Ken Keyes College, 790 Commercial Ave., Coos Bay, Oregon 97420, (503) 267-6412.

Appendix 4

Workshops for Personal Growth

The Ken Keyes College in Coos Bay, Oregon offers a variety of personal growth workshops. Depending on your needs and interests, some are as short as a weekend, many are five-day courses, and some are longer. Weekend workshops are now being offered in the larger cities throughout the United States.

All of the trainings are designed to show you how to break through your personal roadblocks to enjoy your life more fully. The emphasis is on the practical application of the Science of Happiness in your daily life—instead of on knowledge alone.

The lives of more than 20,000 students, businesspeople, teachers, homemakers, counselors, doctors, and others have been enriched by the workshops we have been giving since 1973. Many people come for one training and decide to stay for several. Our participants are discovering firsthand that the Science of Happiness presents methods that work—regardless of the "up-and-down" circumstances in their lives.

Our workshops provide you with practical tools you can use to increase your insight, love, energy, and the joy of living. Group activities combined with individual practice provides each participant many opportunities to explore issues such as relationships, self-esteem, career, parenting, money, health, and opening up one's loving spirit.

We are eager to assist you in discovering ways to create a more satisfying life. The greater awareness and personal empowerment gained in our trainings can help you enjoy increased effectiveness in your life. The skills you learn are yours to keep and use in any situation, so that your growth can continue after the training is over.

These dynamic courses include room, board, and instruction at nonprofit prices that run about one-half the usual cost of other workshops. They are held in an environment offering great natural beauty and recreational opportunities. Across the street from the College are public tennis courts, jogging trails, and a delightful duck pond. Nearby are many attractive beaches; within an hour's drive, there are spectacular waterfalls and the Oregon Dunes National Recreation Area. Located on scenic U.S. 101 on the Oregon coast, Coos Bay is easily accessible by car, bus, or air. We invite you to visit us soon!

For a free catalog of workshops and other courses offered by the College, send your name and address to Registrar, Ken Keyes College, 790 Commercial Ave., Coos Bay, OR 97420. Without charge you will receive a quarterly catalog listing nonprofit workshops, books, audiotapes, and videotapes. If you wish more information about the trainings, you may phone the Registrar at (503) 267-6412.

KEN KEYES COLLEGE
Coos Bay, Oregon

Appendix 5
Other books by Ken

Discovering the Secrets of Happiness: My Intimate Story

Ken Keyes, Jr., $7.95

Here is the inside story of Ken Keyes, Jr., world-known author and personal growth seminar leader. In his frank and touching way, Ken shares his personal search for getting the most out of life. His breakthroughs can help readers recognize their own roadblocks to happiness that may be hidden—even from themselves.

A Conscious Person's Guide to Relationships

Ken Keyes, Jr., $5.95

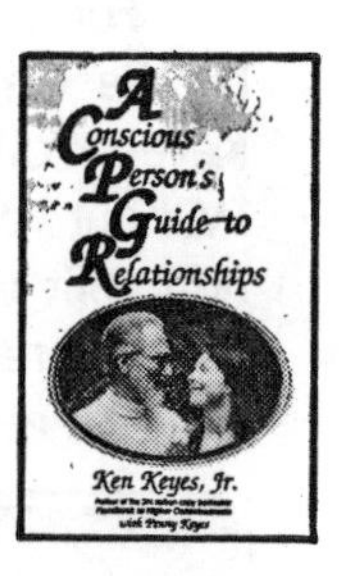

If you're looking for effective new ways to give yourself a love-filled, satisfying, wonderful relationship, you will discover them in this book. Here finally is love without tears! This book contains seven guidelines for entering into a relationship, seven for being in one, and seven for decreasing your involvement with gentleness. It describes sound principles that many people have found invaluable in creating a loving relationship. Over 250,000 in print.

Gathering Power Through Insight and Love

Ken and Penny Keyes, $6.95

Here's how to do it! This outstanding book gives you detailed instructions on exactly how to develop the love inside you. It describes the 2-4-4 system for advancing the transition from the separate-self to the unified-self. These skills are essential for those who want the most rapid rate of personal growth using the Science of Happiness. A vital companion to the *Handbook to Higher Consciousness.*

How to Enjoy Your Life in Spite of It All

Ken Keyes, Jr., $5.50

Each one of the Twelve Pathways has an entire chapter devoted to it. These guidelines offer you detailed insights for creating a more enjoyable life. Step by step, you are shown how to take the Pathways from the printed page and make them dynamic tools for bringing increased energy, perceptiveness, love, and inner peace into your moment-to-moment living. Over 80,000 in print.

Your Life Is a Gift—So Make the Most of It!

Ken Keyes, Jr., $5.95

Presented in a lighthearted, clear style with endearing cartoons on every other page, this charming book shows how to experience fun and joy while at the same time taking responsibility for our thoughts and actions. Geared toward those embarking on personal growth, many folks feel as though it had been written just for them. A delightful gift book.

Prescriptions for Happiness

Ken Keyes, Jr., $4.95

Treat yourself to more happiness by having these three prescriptions handy! They can help you tune-in to your own self-worth—your right to an enriched life—and also help you put more fun and aliveness into your interactions with people. Designed for busy people, this book can be absorbed in a little over an hour. Ideal for gifts. 144,000 in print.

Your Heart's Desire—A Loving Relationship

Ken Keyes, Jr., $4.95

Do you want to bring the magic of enduring love into your relationship? All of us have had a taste of what heart-to-heart love is like. We cherish those times and strive to experience them continuously. Using your rich inner resources, this book can help you to create a more loving relationship—without your partner having to change! 40,000 in print.

Taming Your Mind

Ken Keyes, Jr., $6.95

This book (which has been in print for 35 years) shows you how to use your mind more effectively. It can enormously improve your success in making sound decisions. It is written in an entertaining style with 80 full-page drawings by Ted Key, the famous illustrator. It has been adopted by two national book clubs and there are over 100,000 in print.

The Hundredth Monkey

Ken Keyes, Jr., pocketbook, $2.00

There is no cure for nuclear war—ONLY PREVENTION! This book points out the unacceptability of nuclear weapons for human survival. It challenges you to take a new look at your priorities. With the intriguing concept about the power of our combined efforts, it shows how we can despel old myths and create a new vision to save humanity. Over one million in print.

PlanetHood

The Key to <u>Your</u> Survival and Prosperity

Benjamin B. Ferencz and Ken Keyes, Jr., pocketbook, $2.50

This stimulating book, which is the sequel to *The Hundredth Monkey,* explains how you can give yourself and your family a future in this nuclear age. Don't miss this workable, practical, and urgent way to rescue yourself. 220,000 in print. Receiving enthusiastic worldwide acclaim.

Available in bookstores or from the Ken Keyes College Bookroom, Dept. HB, 790 Commercial Avenue, Coos Bay, OR 97420. Include the shipping and handling fee of $1.50 for the first item and 50¢ for each additional item. You may order using VISA or MasterCard by phoning (503) 267-4112, or you may use the handy order form on page 220.

Two powerful workshops on tape!

Handbook to Higher Consciousness

Cassette, $9.95,
approximately 1 hr.

by Ken Keyes, Jr.

Includes a
32-page Mini-Guide to
Higher Consciousness

- One of the most charismatic and acclaimed philosophers of the New Age, Ken personally brings to you on audiotape his modern, practical blueprint for a life of love and happiness.
- Includes a 32-page Mini-Guide to Higher Consciousness that can guide you toward a vibrant, loving, happy, and fulfilled life!
- If you've had enough of the up-and-down roller-coastering between pleasure and pain, then you are ready to use and apply these step-by-step methods to improve your life while you live it!

Gathering Power Through Insight and Love

$15.95, 2 cassettes

by Ken and Penny Keyes

Includes a
48-page Workbook

- Based on the system used in the popular workshops designed by Ken and Penny Keyes.
- Expanding on the principles found in the *Handbook*, Ken and Penny explain and demonstrate specific techniques that can help you put the Living Love methods to work daily.
- Offers practical and precise ways to develop the skills to radically improve the quality of your life.

See page 220 for ordering information.

Discovering the Secrets of Happiness: My Intimate Story

$7.95

by Ken Keyes, Jr.

- ➤ Inspirational and uplifting book by world-known author and personal growth seminar leader, Ken Keyes, Jr.
- ➤ Explains his own journey from compulsively seeking sex and money to a life of achieving inner fulfillment and consistent happiness.
- ➤ Learn the secrets he uses for creating and enjoying a relationship of "SUPERLOVE" with his wife Penny.
- ➤ Benefit from his wisdom gained through years of life experience and commitment to personal growth.
- ➤ Ken's incredible breakthroughs can help you recognize your own roadblocks to happiness that may be hidden—even from yourself.

See page 220 for ordering information.

See page 220 for ordering information.

TO ORDER BOOKS AND TAPES

Qty.	Item	Price	Amount
	Handbook to Higher Consciousness	$6.95	
	Handbook to Higher Consciousness Workbook Available Spring 1989	$3.95	
	Handbook to Higher Consciousness (Cassette)	$9.95	
	Discovering the Secrets of Happiness: My Intimate Story	$7.95	
	A Conscious Person's Guide to Relationships	$5.95	
	Gathering Power Through Insight and Love	$6.95	
	Gathering Power Through Insight and Love (Cassettes)	$15.95	
	How to Enjoy Your Life in Spite of It All	$5.50	
	Your Life Is a Gift—So Make the Most of It!	$5.95	
	Prescriptions for Happiness	$4.95	
	Your Heart's Desire—A Loving Relationship	$4.95	
	Taming Your Mind	$6.95	
	The Hundredth Monkey	$2.00	
	PlanetHood—The Key to Your Survival and Prosperity	$2.50	
		Subtotal	
		Shipping	
		TOTAL	

Please include shipping and handling charges: $1.50 for the first item, 50¢ for each additional item. **SPECIAL OFFER: If you order 10 items or more you can take off 20%, PLUS we'll pay for shipping and handling.**

☐ **Yes!** Please put me on your free mailing list and send me a free catalog listing workshops, books, posters, music albums and cassettes, and audio and video tapes.

Ship to: (please print) ______________________

Address ______________________

City ______________________

State ______________ ZIP ______________

Telephone No. (   ) ______________________

For VISA or MasterCard orders only:

Card # ______________________

Exp. date __________ Signature: ______________

Send order along with your check or money order to: Ken Keyes College Bookroom, Dept. HB, 790 Commercial Avenue, Coos Bay OR 97420. To order by phone with VISA or MasterCard call: 1-503-267-4112. Call Monday through Friday 9 AM to 4 PM (PST). Allow up to 4 weeks for delivery via fourth class mail.